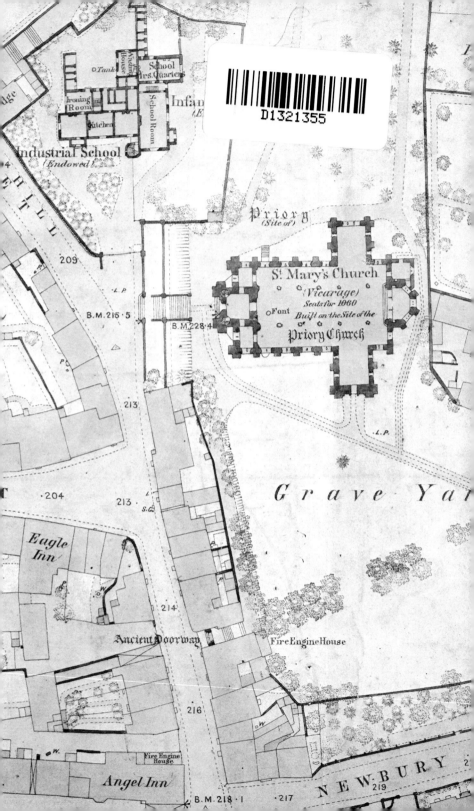

ANDOVER

AN HISTORICAL PORTRAIT

Andover from Ladies walk, 1838.

JOHN SPAUL

ANDOVER

AN HISTORICAL PORTRAIT

WITH DRAWINGS BY
JULIA WHATLEY

ANDOVER LOCAL ARCHIVES COMMITTEE

Dedicated to the people of
Andover, for this is their Town

First published 1977
Copyright © 1977 by John E. H. Spaul
Filmset and printed in Great Britain by
BAS Printers Limited, Over Wallop, Hampshire

CONTENTS

ILLUSTRATIONS AND MAPS

Chapter One
THE FABRIC OF THE PAST

'What's Fame? a fancy'd life in others breath,
A thing beyond us ev'n before our death'.

It is a matter of some regret to many residents of Andover and the Anton valley, that so many otherwise excellent topographical and historical accounts of Hampshire tend to dismiss Andover as a town of no consequence or interest. It is difficult to account for this neglect since on more than one occasion Andover has found itself in the national limelight, and it has always been the principal factor in the growth and development of a large area of Northern Hampshire. On the surface, Andover might appear insignificant to the passing traveller, but beneath its tranquil appearance was a turmoil and a travail comparable with that of any other town.

The feature which distinguishes Andover from so many of its English counterparts and which has prompted and facilitated this attempt to reveal the fabric of its past is the fact that it possesses an unusually rich collection of archives, some of them so ancient that the scratchings of the mediaeval clerks are now barely legible. Fragments of the old feuds, the crooked deals and corruptions as well as the honest everyday business of a mediaeval town, the brief accounts of sober citizens, the criminal records of the hapless labourer crowd the shelves with a challenge to be interpreted. No doubt many other English communities grew in a similar way. What follows may offer interest not only to those who live in Andover, but also to the inhabitants of other neglected communities.

Before any permanent settlement began, the Andover area was important because a major tributary of the River Test was crossed by an essential highway of prehistoric antiquity. Along this track, known between Basingstoke and Weyhill as the Harroway, travelled many groups of primitive peoples; some, no doubt, on their way to Stonehenge; others returning to their homes along the open grassland of the chalk ridges. The Harroway takes a short cut across the Andover basin rather than follow the distant line of the chalk escarpment to the north.

The area was well suited to the life-style of primitive peoples. The open grasslands made movement easy, game flourished in the woodlands on the lower slopes and the clear running shallow streams were full of fish. The stock rearing groups who came along later used the short grass of the chalk uplands for their domesticated flocks of cattle and sheep, and were able where trees were few, to cultivate small plots for simple cereal crops. When the fertility of the immediate area of their temporary shelter was exhausted, the group moved on. There was enough space in the broad basin of the Test river system to accommodate several of these stock rearing groups.

These conditions were equally suitable for the metal using people who followed centuries later. Some of them, the more peaceful, lived in scattered homesteads of a transient nature; the more powerful and warlike built a number of fortified areas on hilltops around the fertile zone. Within this area, and within the present bounds of Andover, Balksbury and Old Down have revealed traces of occupation over a long period, but not of any continuous settlement. Nor did the Romans establish a permanent centre of population here although the neighbourhood is sprinkled with Romano-British farms, some grand enough to be called 'villas', being graced with mosaic floors and furnished with silver vessels. In no case was there ever enough growth associated with the settlement to warrant the use of the term village.

It is quite clear from the archaeological research already completed, that the area drained by the Anton and the Ann was highly developed long before the Saxons came. Unfortunately for those who seek to find a second millenium for Andover's history it is equally clear that no settlement survived the centuries between the end of the Roman peace, and the establishment of the Kingdom of Wessex.

All that survives from the pre-Saxon era is the name of the river, probably Onna-dwfr, or 'the river of the ash-trees'. When one of the Kings of Wessex built a hunting lodge on the spur overlooking the river and conveniently close to the game filled woodlands, it was natural that it should be referred to as 'aet Andefera'. Once royalty had established itself near the river crossing, it was advantageous for traders to spend the night at Andover under royal protection. Royal patronage gave Andover its origin, and royal patronage made it easier for the burgeoning mediaeval town to collect the privileges which ensured its growth.

The Royal Council was occasionally summoned to meet at

Andover when the King was hunting in the neighbourhood. It was at Andover in 965 that King Edgar and his Witenagemot promulgated an ordinance on the proper treatment of the poor, the sick, and the aged. It commended these people to the care of their relatives as a Christian duty and commanded the parishes to see that such care as was necessary was given.

The existence of a church in Andover in 994 is well authenticated. In that year, the Viking Olaf Tryggvason had been persuaded by Aethelred (the King who would not take advice) to abandon an unsuccessful raid in return for 'protection money'. This agreement was ratified by a ceremony in the church at Andover at which Olaf was confirmed by Bishop Alphege of Winchester in the presence of King Aethelred. Hostages were exchanged, and Olaf returned to Norway with an English born bishop and three priests, and within a few years had forcefully converted his country to Christianity, and himself to sainthood. It has been suggested that two local place names with Danish elements, Ibba's farm (Ibthorp) and Thurkel's homestead (Thruxton) indicate where Olaf's hostages settled.

It was by pure chance that such events took place at Andover. Later kings lived elsewhere and were busier, but Andover remained a royal manor. However fortuitous its entry on to the stage of history, the settlement flourished as an agricultural centre and by 1086 when a resources survey was made, its 100 farmworkers could supply the Royal Court at Winchester with food for one day from their own surplus.

It was at this time that a tenuous connection was made between Andover and Saumur. Although the latter town lay beyond the boundaries of Normandy, William I invited the Abbot of St FLorent at Saumur to send three monks to Andover to provide spiritual leadership for the small community. The 'alien priory' or cell of monks under a prior continued to exist, more or less, until it was closed down in 1413 because of the war with France. The last prior of Andover was allowed to give the Priory and its rights to the newly established College of St Mary at Winchester.

Andover might have grown faster if it had not been in the way of the campaigning armies during the civil war between King Stephen and the Empress Matilda. What had begun as a small skirmish between scouting groups turned into a disastrous fire which affected the whole town.

After the war, Andover received royal help in its efforts to rebuilt its economy just as many other damaged towns did. A royal charter of 1175 granting the merchants living in Andover the same rights as the merchants in Winchester possessed, was confirmed by Henry II's sons and grandson, who added such other privileges by other charters that in 1256 it was possible to regard Andover as a town and a borough. It had become a commercial community with a degree of self government, and most importantly, had established an independent existence outside the control of the Sheriff of Hampshire which it was to retain for over six hundred years. As the royal connection diminished, the influence of Winchester College became one of the main factors in the growth of the town until the Gild Merchant developed from a trade protection society into a Municipality.

Repeated outbreaks of fire interrupted the orderly development of Andover. The most serious was in 1435 when almost the whole town was burnt. Only the church and the priory, being built of stone, survived the holocaust. Whereas the rebuilding after previous fires had been a re-occupation of old sites on the hill-top near the church, in 1435 the opportunity was taken to move the weekly market to the lower ground at the foot of the hill, which it still occupies. The accounts of the rebuilding show that specialists were employed. Clerks of works, carpenters, ironsmiths, brick-makers, plumbers, glaziers, tilers, masons, plasterers mentioned in these records show that Andover had progressed from a purely rural economy.

The agricultural strand in the fabric of Andover's past was also flourishing. Sheep were reared increasingly on the extensive downs east of the town, and weavers of cloth established a drying and stretching ground for their products between the market place and the arable field to the east. Wool and pelts were traded overseas, though for some years Winchester was a 'staple town' for wool, and Andover's produce would have been sold there. In Andover parchment makers flourished on the river bank, possibly at the foot of Church Hill.

Throughout this period the Harroway continued to play a major role in bringing traders through the town. It also brought pilgrims *en route* to Canterbury or making their way home, many of whom would have stayed at the Hospital of St John the Baptist at the northern end of New Street. During the Middle Ages, Andover was the third largest town in Hampshire, exceeded only by Winchester and Southampton. Andover's importance did not depend upon the shrine of a saint, but upon the accident of a major trackway. Further chance made Andover a turning point for armies moving along the Harroway, for instance in 1549, 1644 and 1688. The existence of the

Harroway probably also explains why some moderately prosperous London merchants should choose to retire to Andover to play the role of landed gentry which was the ambition of most of their contemporary fellow merchants. The influx of new money with these new men provoked a constitutional crisis within the Gild Merchant which had in any case become too big. In 1415 it had established an executive body of 24 Forwardmen to be responsible for the running of the town, but this system was no longer adequate for a town where newcomers were anxious to take that part in local affairs to which their wealth entitled them, and whose interests might run counter to those of the established gild members. In this situation, reorganisation was inevitable. The Gild Merchant was divided into three Trading Companies whose functions were to license traders in Andover, and to oversee their business methods. In this they were advised by the Earl of Leicester. After Leicester's death the Earl of Essex helped Andover to obtain from Queen Elizabeth a 'Governing Charter' in 1599. From then until 1835 power was in the hands of a self perpetuating oligarchy of twenty four prominent citizens, entry to which could be inherited, purchased or procured by political pressure.

Increased wealth made possible individual acts of charity. Some involved the Free School, established before 1570, and others involved the building of almshouses, or the gifts of 1d. or 2d. loaves. For this was the period when the old, the sick, the orphan or the unemployable were, like roads and bridges, the official responsibility of the parish. While roads and bridges had obvious economic advantages, the others were a liability on the public purse, if not a burden on the public conscience.

There was a strong puritanical element in Andover during the seventeenth century and it was an emigrant from this area, self exiled for conscience's sake, who named the town of Andover, Massachusetts, a name subsequently adopted by other American settlements.

The tide of the Civil War flowed and ebbed through Andover without serious consequence. A 'false Messiah' proclaimed his divinity in Andover, but few were duped and there was no lasting religious effect. The Vicar of Andover who had been expelled in 1648 returned to take his place in the Church in 1660 in a most dramatic fashion. Puritanical ministers expelled from their parishes in 1662 settled in Andover, and held meetings which on one occasional provoked a violent attack; the affair produced a satirical pamphlet.

11

The Corporation of Andover had its own difficulties, particularly those over its own jurisdiction. The wrangle over Weyhill Fair which had its origins as far back as 1562, at its climax involved three jury trials over a period of twenty years, and ended in a Pyrrhic victory for the Bailiff. This affair was complicated by High Tory and Country party factions within the Corporation, and while the former were no doubt jubilant when James II stayed at the Angel in 1688, it was the other side which finally triumphed. A few years later it was accused of corruption by an individual whose punishment was far more severe than that exacted by the House of Commons when on another occasion it found the Corporation guilty of corruption.

Local appointments more than Parliamentary representation were a bone of contention between Corporation and people; on one occasion, there was even physical violence between members of the public and the Approved Men. Despite the conservative attitude of the Corporation, changes were coming to Andover. Improved roads linked Andover with London, Newbury, Devizes, Salisbury and Winchester. Stage coaches stopped and the older inns acquired an added significance. The population of Andover was increased by numbers of coachmen, grooms, ostlers, waiters and cooks. Andover became a favourite halt for some people. On one occasion at least, George III stayed the night at the Star and Garter on his annual journey to the seaside.

The traffic increase, though mainly east-west, suggested that Andover could become a nodal point in the communications system. Clearly heavy goods would need a canal, and one was duly constructed. As it never became part of a through system of canals, it failed to fulfil the dreams of its promoters, though it did bring raw materials for Taskers' Foundry at Anna Valley, and stone for the new church of St Mary.

There was at first no place for Andover in the schemes of the railway planners. 'Andover Road', the nearest station on the South-Western Railway was opened in 1840 eleven miles away at Micheldever. It was not until 1855, thirty years after the opening of the Stockton-Darlington Railway, that the first train arrived at Andover. It followed the winning of the 1854 Derby Stakes by 'Andover' bred by William Etwall, owned by John Gully M.P. and trained by John B. Day at Danebury Stables.

In 1865, Andover was joined by a railway line to Southampton

Detail of early Hampshire map, published by Col. Mudge at the Tower, 1817.

and in 1882 a line to Marlborough was opened to which was added the important branch line to Tidworth.

For many years, Andover has been something of a garrison town. Soldiers from the camps at Tidworth, Ludgershall, Middle Wallop and Barton Stacey and airmen from R.A.F. Andover, established in 1917 with an Officers' Mess built by P.O.W. labour, have made use of Andover's facilities for residence, shopping and night life. Until its closure in 1977, R.A.F. Andover was a sizeable employer of local civilians, and it was granted the Freedom of the Borough in 1955.

As late as 1950, Andover was regarded as a backwater—a place where nothing happened; a place so sleepy and quiet that it was said, no doubt in exaggeration, that the dogs asleep on the pavements were disturbed when anyone stepped over them, so surprising was such an event. One might have supposed that if time had not actually stopped it was moving so slowly as to be imperceptible. But the reality was very different.

Life in Andover was, on the surface, lively. The Mechanics Institute which flourished in the 1880s had its successors in a Debating Society and various other clubs. The Guildhall upstairs, lit by gas which became available in 1838, was the scene of decorous balls, cheerful charity bazaars, noisy political meetings, and stately council assemblies. By contrast the work of the Council's committees became increasing concerned with less attractive matters: outbreaks of swine fever in New Street piggeries, stenches from slaugherhouses behind butchers' shops in the High Street, overflowing cesspools, overcrowded buildings and other nuisances.

Below the Council Chamber, and on the forecourt laid in 1855, well breeched farmers showed samples of their grain for sale every Friday. On other occasions there were auctions of furniture. In West Street, the Electric Picture Hall (established well before 1927 when electricity became generally available in Andover) attempted to fulfil the demands of its noisy audience, noisier still when the film snapped, and the cowboys and indians ceased to spur their horses across the dusty plains. Overlooking the river was the Free Library, equipped with the 'hundred best books' and repeated reminders of 'silence', dingy and unwelcoming, affixed to the walls.

In East Street, the Drill Hall echoed once a week with the barking and stamping of amateur soldiery, recalling the traditions of the Andover Volunteers of the Napoleonic period. Nearby the Fire Engine glistened in its shed while its volunteer crew attended lectures in the Masonic Hall next door. Macabre minded boys peered hopefully at the marble slab in the mortuary in Shepherd Spring

Road. For those whose tastes were more reflective, Mead Hedges was the place to sail boats, to tickle trout, and to gather flags, kingcups and water forget-me-nots. From the High Street, a yellow 'Mobility Bus' left on its staggering, uncertain journey from village to village.

Andover retained its homogeneity, like the villages around it, until destroyed by increasing mobility during the twentieth century, and by the impact of 'total warfare'. Altogether 1099 evacuees, mostly from Southampton were billeted, and 180 bombs were dropped within the Borough boundaries in 1939–1944. The people of Andover retaliated by raising almost a million pounds for war savings, and nearly £8,000 for parcels to P.O.W.s.

There was a possibility after 1945, however, that Andover would subside quietly into the ranks of the larger villages, despite its municipal borough status. Its avoidance of the fate to which it seemed destined, is due largely to the London County Council's desire to relocate some families and factories in areas where growth appeared possible. With the helpful assistance of the Hampshire County Council, a scheme was devised whereby Andover became an expanded town, the development costs being underwritten by the three partners.

As part of the development, new industrial estates were laid out, new housing planned for a three-fold increase in population, new schools, new shops and more social amenities were arranged, and to make it easier to move about, a by-pass was built to the south of Andover, and a spine road arranged to run through the northern areas. From the spine road, an inner ring road enables traffic to service the shops of the new pedestrian precincts. Development did not stop with the Local Government Reorganisation of 1974, although this transferred administrative power to a larger body representing not only the people of Andover, but also the people of the surrounding rural area and other villages and towns in the Test Valley.

It came as quite a shock to many people to find that Andover, after many centuries of municipal dignity and prestige, at a time when it seemed to be growing in wealth and pride, should be merged into a widely enlarged Test Valley District. Yet, as so often in the affairs of men, one person's loss may promote a great happiness in a greater number. What Andover may have lost, the reader will find in the chapters which follow; what it and the Test Valley will gain can only become apparent with the passage of time.

Chapter Two
THE STREETS

'Names, which I long have lov'd, nor lov'd in vain,
Ranked with their Friends, not number'd with their Trains'

ho now remembers Scullard's Lane? No-one does, for it was last used some three hundred years ago. It led to the mill where John Scullard ground grain into flour. More recent memorials to the working men of Andover have been swept away by redevelopment. Pitman's Yard, where a humble blacksmith worked, Telfer's Yard, Joule's Yard which was a builder's, Fouthrop's Yard— he was a cutler—and Alpha Yard have been overlaid. White Bear Yard, King's Yard, White Swan Back Lane, have gone with the inns from which they took their names, and George Yard has grown into a service road for the High Street shops. Streets with meaningful names have gone; few now inspire affection.

West Street is a prosaic name; how much more romantic was the much earlier Frog Lane, or the later Soper's Lane—even if sometimes the S was changed to a T. It matters little, however, for the modern West Street has only the name in common with the earlier West Street, where once the Andover Standard presses thumped, and the picture-goers gathered outside Toni's Cafe. Some old townsfolk can remember Lardy-Cake Lane, running parallel to East Street, although officially its name was changed in 1881 to Rack Close; romanticism was out of favour even then.

Many streets have been known at different times by different names; standardisation and numeration were the product of an increasing postal service and the 1881 census. Competing strongly for the title of 'most named street' in Andover is East Street. A section of this road contained a pond known until 1850 as Scullard's Pond; the rest has been known as White Lane (from the chalk walls of the houses) Shetelane and Back Lane. Straightened in 1968, East Street now has two southern exits into London Street.

Scullard's Lane had almost as many changes. Earlier it was Frog Street; later it became Barber's Lane, Rolley's Lane and finally

Barlow's Lane, as the name of the miller changed. As the northern end of Barlow's Lane became built up it officially changed to South Street.

Dispute is possible over the reason behind Wood Street (or Ward Street) which led eastwards out of the Lower High Street, or Market Place. Was it so called because the houses along it were made of wood, or because it led to the "wood" where the women and children collected fuel for their hearths? There are patches of clay on parts of Bearehill (later Bare Hill, or Bear Hill) where stands of trees could grow naturally. By 1770 the lower part of Wood Street had become part of the London Turnpike Road, and is now London Street.

A turning off Wood Street, first described as Wherwell way, has a complex naming history. It led first to a chalk pit at the southern end of Bere Hill, where later a brick kiln was built which gave its name to Brickkiln Street. In the general improvement of roads in the mid Eighteenth Century the Turnpike Trust used this road and it became part of Winchester Street, as did King's Head Street, which, cut off by a subsequent diversion, became Short Lane and later Dene Lane. The Brickkiln section of Winchester Street superseded by the gentler gradient of the newer Winchester Road became Old Winton Road.

An earlier road led eastwards from the old centre of Andover known as Broadway. Possibly it may have held a market, but stalls and buildings encroached on the space. Then as traffic developed it became London Lane. When the Turnpike Road from Whitchurch and London came into the lower end of the High Street the older road then became Upper London Lane for it led from the Upper Angel Inn. Not for long, however, for dramatic developments led to it being renamed Theatre Street, and after that brief period, Newbury Street. In length it is one of the shortest, but in usage one of the oldest streets of Andover. The rest of Upper London Lane became known as Vigo Road.

A tributary stream of the Anton was known as the West Brook. The street which led westwards across both these watercourses was at various times known as the Westbroke, Duck Street, Gaol Street—since the prison stood near the stream—and today is called Bridge Street. From here Spittal Lane (or Mead Hedges) wound its erratic way along the edge of the West Field to reach the Leper Hospital.

Marlborough Street has also had other names. Before 1860 it was known as Church Hill and as Dogpole Street. Humorists may say that this is derived from the long pole with a noose at one end which was used for catching dogs which had strayed into the church. But such poles are usually made for removing thatch from burning buildings, and the church was an obvious place to keep it. Dogpole is also the name for a section of the marsh at the foot of the hill, where sheep or pigs could be grazed at any time without penalty.

One instance can be quoted of a name being restored. The Black Swan was an inn in the Upper High Street which ceased to exist about 1900. When it became a shop run by Mr. Fox the yard became Fox's Yard; then Rolls' Yard and later still Adams' Yard, but as Freeman, Hardy and Willis Yard was rather a mouthful, the original name, Black Swan Yard, was restored.

The Post Office and the Registrar-General's Department have made changing names a much more difficult affair, and new names are the choice of the developer. So only very few names recall Andover's agricultural past. Acre Path leads from Common Acre across the East or Great Field. Eastfield Road replaces the descriptive Mud Town—where the cottages were built of chalk. Wolversdene is a modern version of Wolvellsdene, a part of the South Field named after John Wolvel (Bailiff 1311). Beside the Anton, Mead Hedges is the meadow for hoggets or yearling sheep. The Drove and the Upper Drove were laid across Charlton Down in 1730, and the Ox Drove in 1785 across Andover Common Down. The Millway, sometimes called Muleway is another reminder of the agricultural past.

Other roads recall features of the past. Chantry Street, one of the few unchanged names, preserves the memory of charitable gifts to the Church in the Middle Ages. Rack Close, a name which has been given at different times to three roads on the edge of the East Field, takes its name from the racks on which the weavers stretched the wet cloth after weaving. Alas, there is no Parchment Street, no Tannery Street and no Silkweavers Street.

Some street names recall individuals. Batchelor's Barn Road takes its name from a barn belonging to Charles Batchelor, Gamekeeper to the Bailiff and Corporation of Andover in the late eighteenth century. Bracher Close is named after W. C. Bracher, a farmer at East Anton, whose family owned the Anton Laundry, and who did much good work in connection with the Mission Hall in New Street. Farr's Avenue is named after a Dr. E. A. Farr, Medical Officer of Health for Andover for many years. As such he was ineligible for election to the Municipal Council, yet so great was the affection in which his fellow townsmen held him that he was elected Mayor for three successive years, 1920–2, and the existence of the War Memorial Hospital owes much to his efforts. Hanson Road—a modern road once called

Mattia's Road—has been deliberately named after John Hanson, an enterprising merchant of the Tudor period. Heath Vale recalled the Heath family of bankers and brewers—their brewery once occupied land between London Street and Winchester Street. Leicester Place is named after the Earl of Leicester, the Elizabethan magnifico whose High Stewardship of Andover deserves recognition. The significance of Suffolk Road is not immediately apparent until one remembers that the eldest son of the Earl of Berkshire and Suffolk is automatically and by courtesy Viscount Andover, a title created in 1622. Portland Grove, and the now extinct Portland Road, recall the frequent visits of the Duke of Portland to the Star and Garter. Being unwilling to pay his bill with coin, he rewarded his host, Richard Bird, with the Lordship of the Manor of Longstock. Shepherd's Spring Lane, might be derived from the seven springs which used to rise in the marshland, or from a Mr. Shefford who worked a mill in that part of the river. Newcomb Close and Goddard's Mead are welcome newcomers to this list.

There are some revealing name clusters. Perhaps the earliest is in the area to the west of Junction Road, known to older residents as 'Victoria Park', where Alexandra Road, Balmoral Road, Osborne Road and Windsor Road meet with Queen's Avenue. The names recall the affection with which Andover celebrated Victoria's Golden and Diamond Jubilees. It would be a mistake to include Albany Road with this cluster, although it is a royal title. The road was named after Duke Leopold of Saxe-Coburg, Duke of Albany, whose personal physician, Dr. G. V. Poore, set out the road for development.

Marchant Road recalls a property developer who lived in Walnut Tree Cottage on the Salisbury Road. He was a prominent member of the masonic craft lodge in Andover, the name of which—St Hubert—was given to the parallel road. Nearby are Wyndham Road, Clarendon Avenue and Lansdowne Avenue, names with masonic connections.

The names Shepherds Row, Sheep Fair Close, Wool Grove, Lamb Close, Bell Road and Pen Close suggest, inevitably, a connection with sheep. These roads were laid out in 1948 on land allotted by the Inclosure Award of 1785 to the Sheep Fair, which was held here until 1870 when all Andover Fairs were stopped. Wellington Road was named after the Grand Old Duke himself, and laid out before 1939, and it is purely coincidental that it runs into Lancaster Close, named after the bomber aircraft of 1939–45. The logbooks of two Lancasters which were paid for with money raised by the Wings for Victory

Campaign in Andover rest in the Archives, while the badge of the ill fated H.M.S. Nestor, reason for Nestor Close, reposes in the museum collection.

It is not possible to omit from a consideration of street names, the Harroway, Port Way, and Icknield Way. The Harroway has had many suggested derivations: hoar way from its chalky surface, hallowed way from its use by pilgrims, but the most likely is 'here-weg' or army way. Its original condition is best appreciated as it drops down through Picket Piece—a name meaning triangular area—weaving from side to side between high hedges. Much of the rest has been obliterated, some by modern roadworks, particularly the stretch known as Drove Meads, or Watery Lane, or the Gulley, so often impassable in wet weather. An earlier alteration of the original route was the result of the Inclosure of Charlton Sheep Down in 1730, and a straightened, cambered, tarred and side-walked section retains the name of the Harroway.

Port Way is an eighteenth century name for the Roman road from Silchester to Sarum. It seems to have been little used during the Roman period, for the Harroway is a much easier route to follow. Parts of its were relaid in the eighteenth century when carriage traffic made it advisable, but the big gaps between these sections indicate its general non-use during the intervening centuries.

By contrast the Icknield Way preserved the line of the Roman road from Winchester to Marlborough far more effectively. It appears inside the Borough boundaries at Picket Twenty—which means a triangular area of thirty acres, as the earlier form Picket-trent-hay indicated—which used to lead into Drunken Tree Drove, a charmingly evocative name for a road of which a small section is now used as a footpath towards the Walworth Estate. Beyond the new houses, the road resumes the character of a country lane passable by pedestrians, if not by motorists, all the way uphill to Chute Causeway. The name Icknield Way was chosen for this road during the Middle Ages, because the King decreed that his peace extended over the Foss Way, Ermine Street, Watling Street and Icknield Way. Though the latter originally ran from Norwich—the town of the Iceni—to Stonehenge, it was used for the Winchester-Andover road, the Salisbury-Dorchester road and the Derby-Alcester road for the added protection which the King's Peace gave to merchants using these routes. A later corruption of Icknield, which is occasionally found, is the equally evocative Hinkering Way.

From the Icknield Way, as it comes over the top of Red Hill, a path along the crest of the ridge south-east of the town was laid out in

1785 as part of the Inclosure Award for the 'publick use and ornament of the Borough'. This path, the Ladies Walk, crossed an old track called Gallicar Way which it was found necessary to lower in 1840 when the road to the railway station at Micheldever was improved. An Iron Bridge was inserted over the Micheldever Road to carry the Ladies Walk, along which trees were planted in 1863 to commemorate the wedding of Edward, Prince of Wales, to Alexandra, Princess of Denmark.

In the northern area of Andover are the names Smannell Road, Enham Lane and Charlton Road, which suggest agricultural practice. Smannell has an unattractive sound, but it is a corruption of Swanhull, found in the 1785 Inclosure Award, and that again is a corruption of Swainhealh. The most likely meaning for this word is the 'healh' or hidden valley, of the 'swains' or young men: probably where the young men were sent to look after the grazing cattle. Enham, or Etham, or even earlier Eanham, is the 'ham' or homestead where the 'ean' or young lambs were reared. This shallow valley would be ideal for lambing sheep. Charlton was the 'tun' or settlement of the 'ceorls' or unfree labourers. Together the three names suggest something of Anglo-Saxon agricultural practice.

One of the most interesting names among the streets of Andover is Newtown Close tucked into the angle between the Weyhill Road and the Millway Road. On one end of a terrace of houses in the Weyhill Road is a tablet recording the start of the construction of Andover New Town in 1858 by John Banks. His planned expansion did not materialise in his lifetime, and only the name records his dream.

Since 1964 a planned expansion has resulted in the creation of a number of residential and industrial estates, only one of which can claim a historical connection. Pilgrims' Way lies beside the route which pilgrims to Canterbury are assumed to have taken from the Hospital of St John at the foot of New Street. Oddly enough, New Street is one of the oldest streets of Andover, being new only when men from Andover went to fight at Agincourt.

A distinction can be drawn between those estates planned as part of the housing expansion programme where some unity of nomenclature provides the estate with a generic title—Floral Way, Admirals' Way, Cricketers' Way, King Arthur's Way, Roman Way—and those areas where development has been haphazard, like the area familiarly known as Spanish Town. The street names reveal nothing of Andover's past, but they will be a reminder to future generations of the amount of building which followed the population explosion of the early and mid twentieth century.

Chapter Three
THE CHURCH

'For Modes of Faith, let graceless zealots fight;
His can't be wrong, whose life is in the right.'

Rearing its early Victorian Gothic elegance above the functional shopping centre, the Church of St Mary dominates the town from its position on the gentle hill top, above the Anton. Its tower is visible for many miles from the north and east, and might appear the only manifestation of the Christian faith in Andover. But there are two other Anglican churches within Andover's boundaries; a very modern Church of St Michael and All Angels lies partly concealed by the Chapel River Press (as if conscious of the decreased role played today by the Established Church), while were it not for its tower, the Church of St Michael at Knight's Enham might be mistaken for an attractive and picturesque cottage. In the tranquility of a secluded residential area lies the Roman Catholic Church of St John the Baptist, and in a more prominent position by the Town Bridge is a Methodist Church; in the High Street is a red brick Baptist Church, a rendered plaster United Reform Church in East Street, a red brick Salvation Army citadel in Winchester Street, a modern Methodist Church, St Andrew's in Weyhill Road and in various locations there are another ten buildings which serve as places of worship.

Despite the number of congregations following differing 'modes of faith', it is still St Mary's which is the dominant building and the only one in Andover to excite that connoisseur of architecture, Sir Nicholas Pevsner. 'A very remarkable building' he called it and one which struck him as 'possibly designed, or conceived or outlined by Dr Goddard himself'. He would have liked 'to know more of the early vicissitudes of this extraordinary and quite brilliant design'.

William Stanley Goddard (1757–1845) had been a chorister at Winchester College in 1769, and later Headmaster. When he resigned from Winchester College in 1809, he came to live in Andover, as he had married a local heiress, though he also had a

London house. As a non resident canon of St Paul's, and of Salisbury Cathedral, and a childless widower after 1830, he was sufficiently rich to 'do a kind act to the parish'. In December 1839 he asked a talented young architect, Augustus F. Livesay, to examine the church with a view to increasing the seating accommodation. The result was the delineation of a new church with a marked resemblance to Salisbury Cathedral. Brilliantly designed though St Mary's may be, its construction has never been entirely satisfactory. The original conception was completed by a steeple, luckily never built as it was considered too heavy for the tower. The facing stones used between the knapped flint walling have weathered badly. The pinnacles were renewed in 1892, the whole stonework treated in 1938 and badly storm damaged portions now have to be replaced once more. Danger notices 'Pass at one's own risk' have been a fairly constant feature of the churchyard. While some admire the grace and beauty of St Mary's, and wish to preserve it, others question whether an Early English style miniature of Salisbury Cathedral in the centre of a commercial district is either well sited or well adapted for the needs of the northern housing estates.

The unhappy conflict is in complete contrast to the unanimity of the vestry meeting at which the present St Mary's was proposed. For many years before 1840 the ratepayers had been subject to a special rate for repairs to the Parish Church. Attempts had been made to persuade Sir John Pollen, who farmed the Priory lands, and Winchester College, the patrons of the living, to repair parts of the church, particularly the chancel. Suddenly on 16th January 1840 at a meeting of the vestry 'for the purpose of receiving certain proposals for increasing the Church accommodation of the parish', the vicar told the twenty seven parishioners present that the tower had been declared unsafe, and that an anonymous donor had offered to replace the whole church at his own cost. The offer was accepted with overwhelming and predictable relief. In fact the result had been foreseen, and, unknown to the vestry, Dr Goddard had already commissioned plans for a new church.

Dedicated with a sermon on the text 'In this house will I give peace, saith the Lord of Hosts', the new church was packed to capacity, which turned out to be less than expected when the decision to demolish the old church was taken. The building of the new church was carried out in stages. The chancel and chantries of the old church were demolished, and the 'unsafe' tower resisted demolition until it was blown up. While services were continued in the nave of the old church, the floor of the new church was laid on arches over the old chancel floor, so that the crypt of the present church contains the gravestones of some eminent personages. Then, when the new nave and chancel were complete, the old nave was removed and a flight of steps made to bring the congregation from the old street level to the new raised level of the church.

Many of the objects in the old church are incorporated in the new. The Kemis monument was restored and re-erected in 1852 and the Venables monument was placed in its present position during the time of Canon Collier. The 'Charity Board' in the South Transept was originally the Benefactions Tablet made in 1692 to refute allegations of corruption. Around the walls of the church have been placed some of the marble memorials of the older church. One noteworthy memorial to Doctor Thomas Coo and his wife Maria contains, in impeccable Latin verse, the bleak message 'Go hence, traveller, imitate while you may the virtues of the dead, for you too must return to dust'. Equally interesting is the tablet to Henry Hulton, First Commissioner of Taxes in Boston, Massachusetts, from 1771 to 1775, whose energetic conduct of his job helped to precipitate American Independence.

Some of the old Church has been preserved elsewhere: the old West Doorway was removed to another site in the High Street where it is now referred to as the 'Norman Gate'; and the handsome chandelier given in 1784 by Miss Mountain is now in Abbotts Ann church. The chief glory of the old church was a magnificent chantry. On the north side of the chancel was a small chantry chapel with an altar to the Annunciation of the Blessed Virgin Mary; on the south of the chancel was a much larger chantry chapel with an altar to St Mary, Our Lady of Pity; so large that it appears to be the chancel and makes the tower appear offset.

The northern chantry was endowed by Peter de Brugge, Sheriff of Hampshire, with lands to the value of £12 for which the priest had to say after every mass, Psalm 130, the morning and evening office for the dead, the 'Commendation' prayers for the dying, and the Seven Penitential Psalms, 6, 32, 38, 51, 102, 130 and 143. The southern chantry chapel was associated with the 'Sandersweved' a combination of a modern friendly society with a trust for maintaining the chapel in which the prayers would be said. A list made in 1469 shows 217 members, headed by William Sandes, Esquire and Margaret his wife.

Elsewhere in the church stood altars to St Sebastian, to St Thomas and a shrine to Holy Cross. In the churchyard stood a separate Lady Chapel and part of its walls and window arches are visible in the

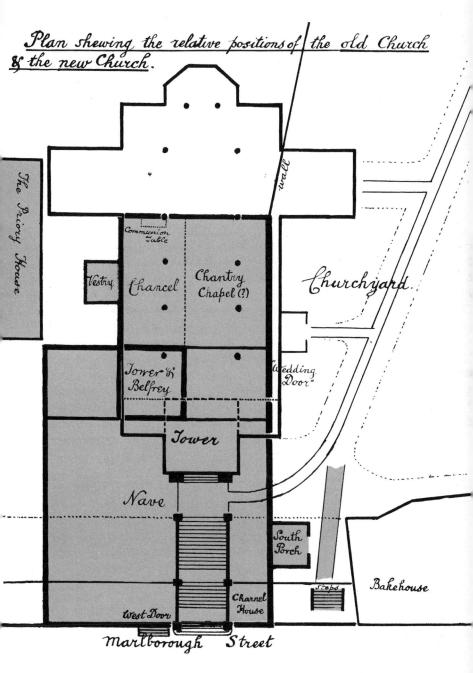

Plan shewing the relative positions of the old Church & the new Church.

The Priory House

Communion Table

Vestry

Chancel

Chantry Chapel (?)

Churchyard

Tower & Belfrey

"Wedding Door"

wall

Tower

Nave

South Porch

Charnel House

West Door

Steps

Bakehouse

Marlborough Street

Plan of the old (tinted area) and new St Mary's Church made by A. C. Bennett.

Shrubbery laid out, in honour of Martha Gale, in Newbury Street. The tower contained a peal of five bells in 1635. There was also a smaller bell which hung in the steeple 80 feet high and 80 feet round the base, which fell on 11 August 1705. The details of this event are recorded in the Churchwardens Book 1677–1721 which was rescued by Canon Braithwaite from a London saleroom.

There is an even earlier set of Churchwardens' Accounts for the years 1470–1472 which were transcribed and published in 1891; as they are some of the earliest for any parish they have a special interest. It appears from these that there was a clock old enough in 1470 to require renewing, and an organ whose bellows were a constant source of expenditure. Inside the church an Easter Sepulchre was a prominent feature, and a roodloft and a 'wedding door'; also banners for use in processions and lamps suspended from the roof before each altar. Also mentioned is a flock of church sheep, for whose washing and shearing the Churchwardens paid 8d. in 1472.

The flock of sheep originally belonged to the Priory which was established at Andover by the Abbots of St Florent at Saumur. A charter granted by Edward II confirmed the original grant (now missing) by William I to St Florent of the church together with 1 hide of land, 13 acres, and tithes—to wit yearly gifts of corn, pigs, sheep, and cattle—and a meadow, and wood sufficient to keep the monks warm in winter, to bake their bread, brew their beer, repair their fences and secure their house from the weather. The monks of the priory were occasionally careless and let their priory burn down. Henry III—a king always beneficent to religious institutions—obligingly allowed them to have forty trees from the Forest of Chute to turn into joists in 1229. Perhaps it was on this occasion that the walls were rebuilt in stone.

During its final 100 years, the priory was in almost continuous trouble. Because of its 'French Connection' it was not allowed to send any profits to its mother Abbey whenever England was at war with France. Instead, the Sheriff of Hampshire collected the profits on behalf of the King; and when the Bishop of Winchester tried to divert this money into his own diocesan treasury in 1341 he was spoken sharply to by Edward III and advised not to meddle. The Sheriff may have been harder to deal with than the distant Abbot of St Florent for the priory began to run into debt. The Registers of William of Wykeham show that the Prior of Andover was cited for non payment of ecclesiastical dues in 1373, and 1385, The Priory was sequestrated for non payment in 1377 and 1393, and the prior of

St Mary's Church, 1838.

Andover was excommunicated on 23 March 1400 for this offence, although he, Nicholas Gwyn, had only just been admitted on 23 October 1399. The excommunication was lifted when the tax was paid, but it was not a situation which could be allowed to continue. In 1413, Andover priory, together with all the other alien priories, that is those with French superiors, was suppressed. The arrangements were made by Nicholas Gwyn, who by royal permission granted the whole priory of Andover in 'pure and perpetuall alms to the Warden and Scholars Clerks' of Winchester College, reserving to himself an annual payment of 52 marks—that is a pension of 13s. 4d. weekly.

The old Church of St Mary was not the first church on the site, though it is not mentioned in the Domesday Survey of 1086. There was a Saxon church, in which Bishop Alphege in 994 confirmed Olaf Tryggvason. Perhaps its destruction in the fire of 1141 when so much of Andover was burnt explains the change of dedication from St Peter—mentioned in Papal Bulls dated 1122 and 1142 (the news of the fire would hardly have reached Rome when the Bull was written)—to St Mary—in a Bull dated 1146. Of St Peter's church only the name survives. If its foundations lie below the present church they are sealed for some time to come.

The Churchwardens' Accounts for 1470–72, already referred to, give a clear indication in financial terms of the practice and rites associated with the Church before the Reformation. Henry VIII's changes appear to have been accepted without question. Edward VI's changes made more visible difference in that all images, paintings and statuettes were removed from the buildings as objects of 'superstition'. The Chantry which had provided Andover with its parish priest was suppressed. Nevertheless some people still clung to the old ways and some very definitely to the new. One who suffered for the new was John Philpot of Thruxton who was burnt as a heretic at Smithfield in 1555 during the reign of Queen Mary.

Queen Elizabeth's compromise solution failed to satisfy John Body, a schoolmaster, who after being condemned at Winchester for denying the Royal Supremacy, was brought to Andover and hanged, drawn and quartered in 1583. Others who refused to accept the new changes took refuge overseas. There appears to be a distinct preference for moderation in Andover and extremism in the villages. Two candidates for admission to the English College at Rome, John Curtis aged 46 in 1609, and Peter Curtis born Andover 1595—but not recorded in the baptism register—had a Catholic grandmother in Longparish and 'schismatic parents' in Andover. The whole family of nine boys and two girls seem to have been religious, two Fathers of the Society of Jesus, two lay brothers, one Poor Clare, and one 'who is a Protestant minister but not malicious, nor (in my view) a bigoted believer' according to John.

In 1625, five recusants in the Andover area, including two members of the Blake family at Enham were disarmed, and their weapons taken over by the local militia. About the same time disappointed puritans were leaving the Andover area. There is evidence of local names in the church registers in Amsterdam, that haven of early non-conformists. Certainly messages by local non-conformist fellowships, later to emerge as 'baptists' were sent to Amsterdam fellowships in the 1620s. When the 'Confidence' of London sailed in 1638 from Southampton she carried the families of Peter Noyce and John Bent, both of Penton.

Amid this confusion of Faiths, for which zealots fought, how was the official Church of St Mary in Andover placed? A survey for the Archdeacon made on 6 June 1635 by Frances Matkyn, Vicar, the Churchwardens and six of the Corporation shows that it steered a middle course. The 'sanctus' bell is equipped with rope and wheel, but the altar is a 'communion table'. 'Two silver and guilt chalices' and 'Three flagons of pewter for the communion' suggest a modest celebration. Two volumes of Erasmus' Paraphrase and two volumes of Bishop Jewell's works stay in the sacristy while 'i Bibell in the largest volume of the last translation', 'ii Divine Bookes and one booke of homilies', 'i booke of marters of a lardg volume' and 'i booke for prayers the 5th of November' are in the body of the church. There are only two surplices and 'one divine's gown for the use of the lecturers', indications that the Vicar of Andover was attempting to keep to a moderate path.

The Reverend Robert Clark was another Vicar of Andover who preferred the moderate path; his story as given in John Walker's *Sufferings of the Clergy 1642–1660* shows his courage, his faith and his tolerant attitude.

It appears to have been loyalty to the King rather than doctrine which was the cause of Mr. Clark's hurried departure. The fact was that he had prayed in public that 'God would infatutate the Counsell of the Parl. and not suffer their wicked imaginations to prosper'.

There was plenty of scope for wicked imaginations as the Revd Humphrey Ellis records in *PseudoChristus* (published in London in 1650). He reveals the whole story of an elaborate charade uncovered at a trial in Winchester. Mary Gadby, a Londoner, began to see visions which she felt were connected with William Franklyn, an Overton boy, who had become a ropemaker in London. She saw him as the 'Messiah' and herself as 'the Bride of Christ'. They came to the Star in Andover, kept by Michael Rutley, and after a fortnight moved on to Mr. Woodward's, the minister at Crux Easton. Here further visions revealed John Noyes to be John the Baptist, Edward Spradbury, a healing angel—from the Book of Revelations—Henry Dixon of Stockbridge and William Holmes of Houghton, two of the destroying angels, and Goody Waterman of Clanville to be the 'King's daughter, all glorious within'.

As an example of religious hysteria, this episode is not unique; examples involving more people can be found in the Puritan colonies of New England. Few of the local worthies took any notice of these visions, and Mary and William Franklyn were eventually accused of bigamy, tried and sentenced to five months while the others were sent to prison pending suitable securities for their good behaviour. The Committee of Parliament had entrusted the conduct of the Church in Andover to Messrs. Leggat and Butcher, a blacksmith and a brazier. They were assisted by soldiers, and sometimes by 'gifted people, particularly one Edward Spradborough, a cloth worker'. Then Mr. Thomas Millett was sent to take Mr. Clark's place. Judging by the fact that when civil marriages were allowed, that is from 1653, most of the couples preferred to have the banns called in the market place, and the marriage celebrated by the Bailiff or a Justice of the Peace, Mr. Millett did not find the situation easy. The end came in 1660. Robert Clark came back from Northleach where he had found temporary refuge, and displacing the minister in mid-service, restored the liturgy of the Church of England and preached 'an excellent sermon on Forgiving Injuries.'

Such were the dramatic events in Andover caused by the Civil War; and there were more to come. Some of the intruding clergy, like Mr. Millett, were expelled in 1660, and others were made to choose in 1662, when the Act of Uniformity forced ministers to sign the Thirty-Nine Articles, or resign. Mr. Samuel Sprint, who was minister at South Tidworth was unable to conform to the liturgy of the Established Church, and in 1662 he retired to Clatford. Two years later, in 1664, the Conventicle Act established a scale of fines for those attending religious services within five miles of a corporate town, except those authorised by the Church. In consequence, the non-conformists met, so says tradition, by night in a dell some four miles from Andover. As no one took much notice, they grew bolder and began meeting in a barn in New Street which was much more convenient for people from all the parishes around Andover.

The leaders of the non-conformist group were Mr Samuel Sprint, and Dr Isaac Chauncy. The latter was the son of the Professor of Greek at Trinity College, Cambridge, who had emigrated to New England in protest at changes in the Anglican Church, before the Civil War started. Isaac Chauncy was enrolled at Harvard University in 1650, and was one of its first graduates, though he came to Oxford to complete his education. He was wise enough to qualify also as a physician so that he could earn a living if, as happened, his congregation disliked his sermons.

The events referred to as 'The New Street Barn Case' began as a result of a meeting on 10 August 1673. On the Monday morning, the Bailiff, John Poppinjay, and two other Justices, Thomas Westcombe, and Peter Blake, fined fourteen attenders 5/- each on information laid by Robert Mooring and Solomon Hunt. They fined Isaac Chauncy £20, for preaching, and Richard Ventham and Phillip Barnard £20 together for allowing the meeting in their barn; and a fine of £5 on Richard Butcher, one of the Constables of Andover, who was present at 'exercising Religion in other manner than is allowed by the Litturgis' and who 'wilfully and wittingly omitted' to inform the Justices. Harsh fines indeed, but it needs more than martyrdom to stamp out non-conformity. On the 8 September the same three justices imposed 5/- fines on another seventeen first offenders, another £20 on Phillip Barnard and Richard Ventham, and 10/- fines on ten second offenders. It seems likely that Samuel Sprint was fined £20 for preaching at that 'seditious meeting', though the charge sheet is missing.

Since many of these seditious attenders at the Conventicle came from outside Andover, it was necessary for the Justices of Andover to ask the Justices for the County to distrain on their goods to the amounts levied or assessed. Before this could be done, Thomas Westcombe seems to have lost his sense of reason, and called out the militia to suppress the meeting in the New Street Barn. Naturally this quickly became a farce, and the whole episode was gleefully written up by an anonymous scribe and duly published with some slight alterations (for instance, Thomas Westcombe became Tom Coxcomb) under the title *Don Quixot Redivivus Encount'ring a Barns- Door in New Street*.

Throughout the whole undignified situation, the churchwardens had refused to charge the non-conformists, and preferred to pay a fine themselves for not doing their duty, rather than cause distress to others. Shortly after the New Street Barn Case, the non-conformists converted the upper floor of a pair of cottages in Soper's Lane, or West Street, into a chapel. Here was a Cox and Box affair, for although the membership of the congregations were very similar, when Mr Samuel Sprint preached it was a presbyterian assembly, and when Dr Chauncy preached it was congregational. There were attempts to unite the two ministers and their followings, but feelings ran very high. Mr Sprint was accused by some of being a Baxterian, that is an occasional conformer and the Revd Joseph Ball, his successor, was accused of Arianism. Toleration for all religious groups was proposed by James II in 1687, and after 1689 the non-conformists could meet openly and without interference. Dr Chauncy left Andover for London in 1687, and when his successor the Rev. Samuel Tomlyns left, there was a move to unite both groups. While the Presbyterians submitted to the authority of the priesthood, the Congregationalists maintained the right of the members to choose their own leader, to be Independents. So the latter opened an Upper Meeting House in East Street in 1700, while the Presbyterians continued to meet in Soper's Lane. On the death of the Rev. Joseph Ball in 1747, his remaining followers reverted to the Established Church and allowed the Presbyterian connexion to lapse.

Another early group of non-conformists were the Quakers who

were taken up and prosecuted for holding a meeting in Andover in 1681. Ten years later the Society of Friends was well established and a meeting house in East Street was built in 1713. Meetings continued to be held there until 1843, but the Quaker burial ground still exists in Winchester Street and is now the responsibility of the Test Valley Borough Council. Early Friends were persecuted by the authorities because of their outspoken criticism of other churches and their non-observance of social customs which they believed to be wrong.

In 1751 John Wesley passed through Andover without preaching; he returned and gave sermons on 2 November 1759 and 7 November 1760. In consequence, a Methodist chapel was erected on the corner of Shepherds' Spring Lane and New Street, and became the centre of the Andover Circuit in 1817. A new chapel was built in 1820 on the site of the Royal Oak in Winchester Street. Meanwhile a section of the East Street Independents who were of the Baptist persuasion (Baptists were very strong in Whitchurch where other non-conformists were thin on the ground) separated themselves and built a chapel in the High Street which opened in December 1824. More faiths were added soon afterwards when the Primitive Methodist group invaded the Wesleyan Methodist territory. On 5th May 1833 they held a meeting at the Walled Meadow where the opposition resorted to egg throwing and other methods of intimidation. Nevertheless, the Primitive Methodists established a chapel in East Street in 1836 and founded a circuit in 1837.

In the Baptist Church in the High Street—rebuilt in 1866—there was between 1875 and 1881 a sad and at times a bitter controversy over the use of wine at Communion Services. Since the founding of the fellowship the wine had been one of the fermented variety, but such was the feeling of the times when Andover's Temperance Hall and various temperance inns were established that a dual system prevailed for a time, abstainers taking unfermented grape juice.

In the late nineteenth century religious revival took a number of forms. The ranks of the Methodists had been swelled by a number of wealthier citizens, who wanted a more prominent building. The new Methodist Church was built next to the river in Bridge Street and opened on 19 April 1906. The old building in Winchester Street was sold to the Salvation Army as their citadel, their older building in New Street being rather small.

The Roman rite had been observed since the repeal of the Test Acts in 1829, and the small congregation in Andover used a room at the back of the Station Hotel, above some storerooms. It was approached by a wooden staircase and one wall formed part of the boundary wall of the Old Town Station. During the twentieth century, the Roman Catholic congregation moved to a brick church in Weyhill Road, which was rather uncomfortable in hot weather for the roof was corrugated iron. Fund raising for a more suitable church took some time, but finally the Church of St John the Baptist was opened in Alexandra Road in 1958. It is a simple but impressive building in red brick with a wood and plastered front. Inside, the vaulted wooden ceiling is carried on eight fluted granite pillars and lit by stone-mullioned windows rising from floor to roof. Church rooms for other occasions have been added more recently.

With the spread of housing along the Weyhill Road, it was felt by the Methodists that another church was needed to cater for the new population. The result was St Andrew's, an unpretentious building but one that has proved useful not only for holding Services for Worship, but also for providing accommodation for a Play School for small children in that area. For a similar reason a new Anglican church was built behind the Chapel River Press; this was an all-purpose hall to serve a 'Conventional District' in the first instance, but in May 1960 it became a full parish of St Michael and All Angels, and a new church was completed in 1964. This is dismissed by Sir Nicholas Pevsner as 'brick with a central spike', but Mrs Margaret Green in *Hampshire Churches* described it as 'perhaps the most architecturally stimulating building ... where the tall clear windows, east and west, achieve a sparkling, light-filled interior crowned by a yellow painted ceiling which seems to float overhead like a canopy of geometrical shapes from which clusters of dark shaded lights descend'.

The Society of Friends began to meet again in Andover in the 1940s, and many other religious groups mainly Christian and limited in numbers have established themselves in Andover. To counteract this diversity, a Council of Churches in Andover, on which all the main religious groups in the town are represented, has done much to develop the sense of unity though as organisations, the churches remain separate. On the new estates, and especially on Cricketers Way, the first estate north of the railway and therefore more cut off from the town, the various churches have combined to provide Services for Worship in the Community Centre.

Nevertheless despite attempts at unity and compromise, as well as attempts to introduce breakaway groups, for strangers to Andover and for many of Andover's own people it will be the tower of St Mary's which will remind them that the origin of Andover is to be found in the early Christianity of the Saxon Kings of Wessex.

Chapter Four
THE TOWN MILL

'Safe on my shore, each unmolested swain
Shall tend the flocks, and reap the bearded grain;'

nlike St Mary's Church which stands proudly for all to see, the Town Mill has hidden itself behind a variety of disguises, at times a private dwelling, a restaurant, a dental surgery, Youth Club, Advice Centre, and more. Its origin is plain to pedestrians crossing its front who glance upwards and notice the tablet commemorating its restoration by Sir John Griffin Griffin K.B., M.P., (later Lord Howard of Walden) when John Pugh was Bailiff of Andover 1752–3. One of the reasons why the Corporation chose Sir John to represent Andover was his generosity. Who else would provide a large part of the capital necessary for the reconstruction!

For over 900 years there has been at least one mill in Andover. In 1086, when William I's officials made enquiries about economic resources, there were six mills. The position of only four mills can be given with certainty. Cricklade Mill had been disused for many years; the Town Mill still strides the river; Anton Mill (previously known by the names of successive millers, Barlows and so on) has become an engineering works; Rooksbury Mill, the lowest on the river has been both a pig and mink farm. The six mills had an annual value in 1086 of 72/6d. They ground the corn grown by the sixty-two villeins, thirty-six bordars and possibly the three coliberts and six serfs who made up the adult male total. To help them plough the fields, they had the use of twenty-four ploughteams; that is to say a total of 192 oxen. By comparison with other villages the ratio of oxen to labourers is high; if each team ploughs one acre for twenty days in the autumn and twenty days in the spring, the arable acreage would be nearly one thousand. Unfortunately, the Survey of 1086 does not record the amount of land in the royal manor of Andover—whether the clerk made a mistake in copying from the rough draft, or whether the surveyors could not persuade the men of Andover to disclose the extent, will never be known. By the time that records were kept there were four arable fields in Andover, the North Field, the West Field, the South Field and the East Field, and two fields in Charlton, the South Field and the West Field. In addition there was a large Common Down east of the East Field, and a Sheep Down to the north of Charlton's Fields.

Today, fields are identified by numbers on large scale Ordnance Survey maps, or by Grid References, and can be recognised by the hedges or fences which enclose them. In earlier times a field contained many pieces of land identified by 'familiar' names. In the Andover fields some of those names reflected the type of terrain, Stony Furlong (1411); some its position in the field, 'Medforlang (1285) or Longefurlonge (mediaeval) or Cherrywell Bottom. Others recalled a family name, Wollvesdene (1585) Mortrell's Pasture (1649) Tottesmeade (1342) Dimnokeslade (1373).

Humbler folk are commemorated in such names as Sokeners (1409). Other names refer to a feature; Hethenfeld (1330) contained round barrows which were recognised as burial mounds of a non-Christian variety. Strecche (1340) may well refer to a place where cloth was stretched in its final stages between tenter-hooks. Other names for imaginative reflection are Estbovedon (1322) and Suthebovedone, Bottocks, (1332) Poulland (1373) Annahamdone (12th century) 'la flode' (1266) Harenhagge (1311) Pepers Orchard (1649) Maydynhalve (1467) and Hollam's Breach.

Manorial customs are basically identical, though there are variations between manors. In Andover there is very little evidence for manorial customs, but in 1465 it was ordered 'that no man woman or childe Rake yn ony mannes land ane Corne yn harvestyme ne after with no Rake'. Gleaning by hand was permitted but the use of even a simple machine like a rake was forbidden. A tattered sheet of Presentments or Accusations for 1570 ordered 'that thei that have kyne to goe in the mershe shall aswell yf their kyne goe in the mershe to paye the koweherd' that no 'persons shall put or cause to be put into the mershe or mershes belonginge to the town of Andover any hoggs or piggs', that 'no hoggs shall come into the market upon the market days'.

Another set of presentments for a hundred years later has similar hints of customs; on 27 April 1693, the jury presented Isaac Cooper for 'feeding his Cows in the hog marsh contrary to the custome'. On 5 October they presented 'Robt Grace Abram Kent Richd Herne Thomas Mealy the sheppards for Bringing the Sheep Belough Hill before Michaelmas Being a breach of a former custome' and ordered 'that the sheppards shall keep no sheep on clovergrass sown Belough hill from the first of March tell Michaelmas and from Michaelmas to the first of March it shall be common', and that 'the Hayward shall have for the pounding of Townsmens Cattell no more than one penny and of A farrinnar foure pence'. On 18 July 1695 'We prasant & order that noe Hoggs nor piggs shall goe into the Cow Mash'. On 23 April 1696, it was ordered amongst others that 'no cattell should or ought to be fed in the drove till Whitmunday'; that 'in May & August the flock of Sheepe that are kept in the Common be told over to see if thereacend more Sheepe than theire land will maintain & for every Score of Sheepe that are kept by any person or persons more than he or they have Common for to paye five shillings a month', that 'noe person shall keepe hoggs in the field att Harvest till the Corne be carryed in out of the feild or the feild broke with the parsonage Hoggs'.

These orders are mostly for good husbandry, but also in part to preserve individual rights in the common field. As there are many cases of individuals having rights on the common or waste land without having any rights in the arable fields, it would be unjust to allow non-arable common right holders to pasture their animals on the stubble of the grain-growers. The right to 'break' the field after harvest normally belonged to the Lord of the Manor—the Corporation of Andover; but since William's charter to St Florent included 'from his own pasturage, one pig, and a meadow of 12 oxen and a flock of sheep', it is likely that the Lord's right was transferred first to the Priory, then to Winchester College and its chief tenant, who farmed the Parsonage. After the gleaners, the parsonage flock would be in to break the surface of the fields, thus making the subsequent ploughing easier.

The wheat and barley produced in these fields provided food and drink for the workers. Indeed the abundance of barley gave rise much later to a local brewing industry, though the making of small beer was an essential part of domestic economy in the Middle Ages. Wheat, however, needs to be ground before it can be used, and the provision of a mill for grinding corn was the privilege and duty of the Lord of the Manor. The presence of six mills, suggests six sub-manors, but this presents difficulties of identification.

By 1291 one of the mills had become known as 'la tunmulle'; and it was here that most men brought their wheat for grinding. The expense of building the mill with its weir and leet, and fitting the heavy grinding stones was recouped from the tolls paid by the farmers. Sometimes these tolls were too high. In 1379 John Lytelmulward (the-town-mill-warden) was fined in the Hundred

Court for taking an unjust toll. In 1510, the Town Mill is described as a 'vacant place'. Did angry customers take revenge upon an unjust miller by burning his mill, or was it burnt by accident, blown down or carried away by floodwater? The Merchant Gild of Andover did not wish to pay for a new building, and so leased the site to Richard Asheton for an annual rent of 5/-, with the right to rebuild. Richard died in 1530, and his son John sold his rights in the mill to Richard Gilbert of Andover, a mercer, who without delay obtained a conveyance of the ground from the Merchant Gild, thus securing complete title to the Town Mills which are described as being lately built by Richard Asheton.

The miller continued to be a target for his fellow-townsmen. At the Sessions held at Andover on 8 June 1598, William North, a miller, was fined 3/4d. because he took excessive toll in weight, viz. 7 lbs toll for grinding one bushel of grain when he should have taken but 2 lbs and not more as provided by Statute. He was also fined 5/- for keeping divers pigs and fowls at his mill 'for robbing the grain of Her Majesty's subjects which is brought to be ground'.

In 1601 the Town Mills are described as being two mills under one roof, one for grinding wheat, the other for grinding malt. The Corporation was regretting its sale, and took the opportunity given by an endowment to purchase the Town Mills for £170. From then until 1904 when the Borough of Andover sold them, the story of the Town Mills can be traced in the Minute Books, the Account Books, and the vouchers for work carried out. A recurrent expense was the purchase of new grinding stones. A pair of 'cullen' or 'Cologne' stones were purchased in 1731 to replace stones removed by the previous tenant. Then in 1752 the mill was repaired and extended at the expense of General Sir John Griffin Griffin.

While an early form of agriculture involved both animals and grain crops, it was particularly important that on the thin soils of the Hampshire Chalklands sheep and grain should be worked together. It was necessary for every village to have a 'sheep-walk' where the sheep were pastured during the day. At night the sheep were brought down to the arable land and folded between hurdles in one of the Open or Common Fields. Here their presence would restore some fertility to the field in the form of manure. During the winter, when grass was not growing, the feed for the sheep would be the hay made during the summer from the grass of the low-lying manorial meadows in the valley bottom. Peculiarities in the boundaries of the parish are due to the need for each village to have some of each type of land within its own limits.

In Andover the sheep-walk was on the Common Down to the east of the town. There was also a sheep walk for Charlton which lay north of the village. There was also a large amount of woodland, especially to the north-east and a considerable amount of waste. A survey was made in 1691 of the lands and tenements in Andover. It began with considerable detail listing the owners of tenements and lands in the arable fields giving exact acreages and location. Smaller landowners' holdings are totalled but not divided between the fields. Adding up all the amounts given, there are 226 acres in the West Field, 372 in the South Field, 287 in the East Field and 209 in the North Field, with 470 other acres of arable and probably about 130 of meadow. There were a number of enclosed farms—Sottwell's or Seymor's Farm consisted of 180 acres—there was also the Parsonage Farm which was valued with the tithes at £150—possibly this represents another 200 acres—New Street Farm, valued at £50 should account for a further 200 acres; and there was a further 103 acres of town land in the arable fields. As this total amounts to about 2,400 acres it is probably an accurate estimate of the total farmland of the period.

The pattern of farming changed in the seventeenth century when exiles returning from Holland brought new ideas for crops and methods. One of these new methods was the 'water-meadow', a field which could be 'floated' or 'drowned' with water from the river, and then drained. This way of warming the soil early in the year produced a crop of grass for ewes and lambs before the sheep-walks were capable of feeding them. Irrigating the fields in the early summer after the initial grass-feed meant an early hay crop, and yet a third crop of grass late in the season. The water-meadows were made first in the Itchen valley soon after 1660, but were copied in the Anton and Test valleys before 1700.

New crops were also introduced, rye-grass, sainfoin, clover and turnips; the later reduced the winter-feed problem, and together they made the need for a sheep-walk less vital. Some time just before 1700, possibly in 1692, proposals were made to plough half of Andover Common Down and turn it into arable; the price of wheat was rising and an increase in arable land would be profitable. After four years of being sown with wheat, during which time the fertility of the Common Down would be exhausted, it was to be sown with grass. For the next five years, the other half of the Common Down was to be ploughed and sown likewise. The proposal was made and considered seriously; the draft agreement was almost completed except for the concluding formula and the date.

If Andover Common Down could not be turned into arable land, there were other places that could. In 1730 all the Charlton fields and down were inclosed by a private agreement among the holders of 'stints'—rights to graze sheep—because 'the Sheep Down was generally overcharged with sheep'. The three Commissioners chosen by the stint-owners awarded 802 acres in 94 allotments to 48 different proprietors in amounts ranging from 132 acres to less than one acre. Unfortunately, there were complications arising from a sudden death, and after a petition and a counter-petition, an Act of Parliament was given the Royal Assent on 29 April 1740 to confirm the Award made on 14 November 1730. Some details—like names, and acreages,—are missing from the Act because of the time lapse involved. Some of the villages around Andover had already inclosed their fields and made small farms of their own. Others followed inclosing either the whole or part of the Common Fields, by agreement among the landowners.

A change came when Abbotts Ann was inclosed by private Act of Parliament in 1775; the difficulties caused by inheritance were at the root of this radical solution whereby, provided eighty per cent were in favour, the remainder would have to give way. In 1784 the freeholders of Andover who wanted Inclosure succeeded in securing an Act of Parliament to inclose 2120 acres of arable land in Andover Common Fields, Common Down and waste land together with 833 acres in Enham Heath and Finkley Down. Since then, except for the removal of hedges and town development, the field pattern of Andover has remained relatively unchanged.

The Bailiff and Corporation as Lords of the Manor and Owners of the Soil of the Downs and Waste were offered a fiftieth part for those rights, but held out for a fortieth. Since they received 15 acres for them, the Common Down must have been about 600 acres in all and the Common Fields 1520. The land was redistributed in 169 lots; the Corporation received seven lots including two chalkpits, a four acre piece for a fair and about 77 acres of land for the Town and 70 acres for the Charities. The major landowner was Winchester College. John Pollen, who as a freeholder of Andover was allotted 175 acres, worked the Parsonage Farm—a farmhouse converted from the old Priory Cloisters—for the College, which was allotted 68 acres of land. Another of the College's tenants, Alexander Willis was allotted 125 acres as a freeholder, and 100 acres as the tenant of Calley's Farm which was situated in the angle between New Street and Vigo Road. The third tenant, William Saunders, received 18 acres on his own account, and 47 acres as the tenant of Chantry Farm which was at the foot of Chantry Hill.

When W. H. W. Titheridge examined the Corporation documents in 1837 he reported that the Inclosure Award was already illegible in a number of places and almost so in the rest. The original having now completely disappeared, two copies one enrolled in the Quarter Sessions Order Book, the other made by William Burrough Child in 1822, supply details of these allotments. A map of the allotments in the East and South Fields and Common Down has survived, but this was itself a copy of a portion of the original map. Enough details are given in the award, however, to enable the remaining allotments in the West Field, Enham Heath and Finkley Down to be identified with existing fields.

There was a short period of adjustment after the Inclosure Award, and the Corporation experienced some difficulty in letting its new fields on Andover Down, partly because there were no existing buildings and erecting these and the hedges had to be done by the tenant. An attempt to lease 50 acres of good arable and 50 acres of good 'maiden down' for a fine or premium of £300 at an auction reached only £30 per annum. Later, Jere Bunny offered £35 rent, if his lease could be renewed twice at a £25 fine since he would have to spend £200 on buildings. The Corporation also offered him, and he accepted, a lease of 70 acres on the Common Down at £23.10.0d. for the first year since he had to erect the fences, and £33 for the next twenty-nine years.

In the nineteenth century payment of tithes became a source of tension between the incumbent and the cultivator as the profits of an acre rose and the costs of living rose also. Accordingly, later than in many other parishes, the Tithes of Andover were commuted, that is changed to an annual money payment. The Award was made by William Wakeford an Attorney on 9 May 1848 and he calculated the Vicar's Rent Charge at £570, while Winchester College, as successor to the Prior of Andover, was awarded £1674.2.10d. The award was apportioned by Giles Westbury of Andover and Richard Gale of Winchester and signed by them on 12 May 1848. The acreage of the whole Parish including Wildhern, Hatherden, Knights Enham and Foxcot, according to Wakeford was 7,453 acres of arable, 113 acres of meadow, 351 of Pasture or Downland, and 598 of woodland. Only two plots, Little Farthing Meadow ($1\frac{1}{2}$ acres) and Knights Enham Glebe (3 acres) were not subject to tithe. In the event, since Sir John Walter Pollen was the lessee of the Warden of Winchester College, and of the Vicar of Andover, he received an annual income of £2,220, the remaining £24.2.10d being paid direct to Winchester College.

The map made in connection with the Tithe Commutation Award is the first complete map of the Parish of Andover. For each of the 1941 numbered plots of land, there is named the owner, the occupier, the nature of the land and the amounts payable.

One interesting set of entries relates to William Hawkins Heath who is shown as owning and occupying Vigo Lane Farm, with Yard, Barns, Cottage and Buildings, a Bank-house with Barn and yard and a large House, Garden, Stables and Malthouse. The latter was probably his own residence and the malthouse for his own use, because he is also the owner of a Brewery and Yard, the Catherine Wheel Inn, Yard and Buildings, the Bush Inn, Yard and Buildings, the Rising Sun Inn, Yard and Buildings, and the Red Lion Inn, Yard and Buildings. He owned 85 acres of arable and four acres of meadow, and another ten houses which he rented probably to his work force. This is typical in that Gentlemen Farmers usually had other occupations to follow like banking and brewing, and it makes it clear that Andover was still very much a collection of farms with a shopping area in the middle.

The period which followed the commutation of tithes is generally regarded as the time of 'high farming' when large profits were made. Unfortunately the details of this period for any farm in Andover are not available, but the farm labour accounts for Eastover Farm at Abbotts Ann show that Andover was a natural centre for selling grain, both wheat and barley, and pigs, and for buying guano and coal. The former when mixed with other materials, possibly including lime or chalk from Andover chalkpits, and dung from the stockyard was used as a fertiliser; coal was necessary for the steam threshing machines which were then available, some being produced locally at Taskers Brothers' Foundry in Anna Valley. These farm labour accounts are extremely full. They were kept by a new tenant of the Eastover Farm on the Red Rice Estate, who came to Abbotts Ann from Norfolk, and being a careful and thoughtful farmer recorded in detail the first years of his tenancy. Especially interesting are his attempts at chemical fertilisation, in view of the recent establishment of the Rothampstead Agricultural Centre.

But the boom in farming seems to be over by 1870; the period of 'high farming' on the Hampshire Chalklands should be dated before, rather than after 1850. The introduction of improved breeds of sheep, the Southdown, and the Southdown-Hampshire cross resulted in an improved crop of wool and a quick fattening lamb. Sales of sheep at Weyhill Farm rose steadily for some years and a wool market held in Andover in 1846 for the first time resulted in the

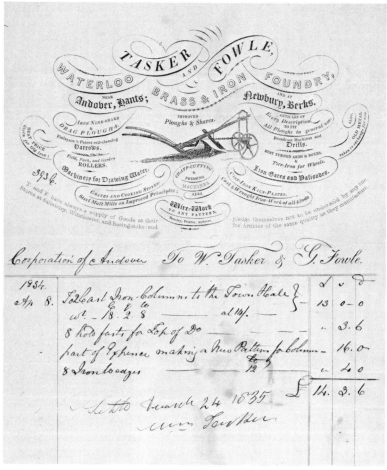

Billhead, 1834, showing wide variety of new agricultural machinery available locally.

sale of 12,468 fleeces. Despite advertisements in the Bradford papers, the sale never again reached that amount. The public were becoming more conscious of health, too, and a Contagious Diseases of Animals Act was passed in 1868. Thereafter the records of Andover's Municipal Corporation is spotted with references to swine fever, and foot and mouth. On 26 November 1870 rules were made to contain the outbreak of foot and mouth disease from which Mr Holloway had lost one cow, and in July 1882 there was an outbreak of swine fever which affected 13–18 Vigo Road and 56–60 New Street. More exciting, though less dangerous, was the appearance in the streets of Andover on 16 June 1877 of a rabid dog—probably sunstroke rather than rabies virus. Later the Corporation recorded its thanks to a Mr Stagg for the promptitude and energy he displayed in following and securing the dog believed to be mad.

With the appointment of an Inspector of Contagious Diseases, the Parish pound, where stray cattle and sheep had been impounded until the fines were paid, became of less importance. Earlier repairs to the Pound are frequently mentioned in the accounts of the Town Chamberlain. More often the condition of the Pound was notified to the Corporation. The last occasion appears to have been in 1869 for an investigation of the condition of the Pound was ordered on 1 May 1869. On 9 November 1871, the Council agreed to repair the Pound, and it was completed by 3 February 1872.

In view of the decline of 'high farming' in the late nineteenth century, it is surprising to find the Wiltshire Agricultural Show being held in Andover in 1895 and again in 1903. Andover Sheep Fair had started in 1876 to replace the earlier fairs, and this continued to run as a Show, with prizes, as well as a sale ring until 1939.

One special development of the twentieth century was the creation of a Land Settlement Association originally for unemployed miners, and later for ex-soldiers in 1919. One area selected for these purposes was in Little Ann, on land adjoining the old West Field. For many years the L.S.A. supplied the people of Andover with market garden produce, and though now technically wound up, the smallholders still grow strawberries and other fruits and vegetables in large quantities. There were some cress beds in the river at the foot of Marlborough Street, as there were elsewhere in the valleys of the Bourne and the test. The cress beds no longer exist for the area has been scheduled for redevelopment.

Many of the changes in farming in the twentieth century can be parallelled elsewhere in England. Most of the Common Fields are built over, and building has even encroached on the Common Down. Water meadows have been drained and used for other purposes. The old mills on the river bank are abandoned as new methods of milling are introduced elsewhere. The Town Mills are now put to uses which John Lytelmulward would have found absolutely incomprehensible, but so long as they remain visible to the passing motorist, or the car park user, they will serve as a reminder that, although a stranger might judge Andover to be eminently commercial in character, the town has a long agricultural tradition, and whatever industrial activity or commercial facilities it enjoyed were in fact an expression of its farming past.

43

Chapter Five
THE MARKET

'At early Morn, I to the Market haste,
(Studious in ev'rything to please thy Taste)
A curious Fowl and Sparagras I chose,'

Not everything can be found in Andover's Saturday Market. One might wait a long time before finding asparagus or 'curious Fowls' among the more ordinary objects displayed for sale. Fish, fruit, vegetables, meat, eggs, cheese, plants, carpets, clothes, shoes, china and antiques are sold in the High Street between 8 a.m. and 5 p.m. on Saturdays. The land on which it held is part of the 'waste of the manor' bounded on the east by a section of a County road, the A343, Newbury to Lopscombe Corner, and on the west by a District road, part of the High Street. Until the recent closure of the Upper High Street to cars and the creation of the new Shopping Precinct which blocked one exit from the High Street, Saturday morning was a nightmare for drivers. Shoppers, too, as they dodged from stall to stall, narrowly avoided collisions with the Winchester-Newbury traffic as well as the double-decker service buses.

There is an air of eternity about Andover market as though it had always been there. In fact, the situation was created in 1947, when the market was moved back to its original site and to its original day. Two immediate results of this change were a 2,000 per cent increase in rents paid by street traders, and the appointment of a Market Supervisor. The approach of war in 1939 had caused misgivings in the minds of the authorities, and it was decided to move the market—then held on Friday—from the High Street, first to the Walled Meadow—found to be too wet—and then to the Sanitary Yard off Bridge Street where the Corporation built a roof over the site of the fatstock market which was held there on Mondays.

Saturday was the day specified in the 'Great Charter of 1599' for holding a market. It was changed to Friday in 1857. Printed Rules were issued for the conduct of a weekly Corn Market between 12 noon and 2 p.m. and a Cattle Market on the First Friday of every month between 10 a.m. and noon. In 1879, despite a petition against it, the Town Council decided to spend not more than £25 on movable cattle pens so that sheep and cows could be auctioned in the Market Place. There was also a pig market, held until 1864 behind the Eight Bells Inn (now the Station Hotel). When the Railway needed the land for the Town Station, Mr Shere of the Masons Arms Inn applied for the lease of the pig market, which was granted to him at one guinea annual rent for the privilege.

That there was a need for a market is clear from a petition drawn up in 1870 by the grocers and other shopkeepers protesting about hawkers who tried to sell fruit and vegetables in the street at all hours and on any day, and asking that stalls should be set up for the sale of perishables in the Market Place on Wednesdays and Saturdays only. The petition was presented in February 1871 to the Mayor as successor to the Bailiff who was also Clerk of the Markets by the authority of the 'Great Charter of 1599'. On taking office as Clerk of the Market, he swore to 'forsee that the juste and trewe assises of Bread and Beare and Wyne be dewlye kepte And that all manner of victualers Butchers and fishemongers doe sell good and wholesome victuals and all reasonable prises without excesse'.

No Bailiff could carry out all these duties and others in person, and some of them were carried out by deputy; one of them took the 'Aletester's Othe' namely to 'well and trewely see from time to time that the Bread brought to be sold within this Towne be dewly wayed and that the same contayne in weight according to the prises of Corne in this Markett . . . Also . . . all the Brewers and Tiplers within your office . . . doe make good and wholesome Ale and Beare for men's bodyes, And that they shall not sell any before the same be tested by you . . .'

To help the Aletester to see that the bread sold in the market was of the correct weight, a special list of weights and prices was made out, and a fourteenth century copy of this Assize of Bread is one of Andover's prized records. By the Statute of Winchester 1285—an enactment substantially in force for the next 500 years—the price of the various types of loaf, described as the 'ferthing wastell', the 'ferthing whyt loffe', the 'halpeny whyt loffe', the 'halpeny Whettyn loffe', and the 'halpeny loffe of all maner of grayne' remained constant, while the weight of the loaf, whichever it was, varied with the price of corn. There were no standard weights and measures in those days, so the weight was calculated in silver coins. For example, when the price of wheat was 10/- per quarter, the halfpenny wheat loaf was to weigh the same as £1-11-3 in silver coins. Andover's copy of the Assize of Bread testifies to one of the

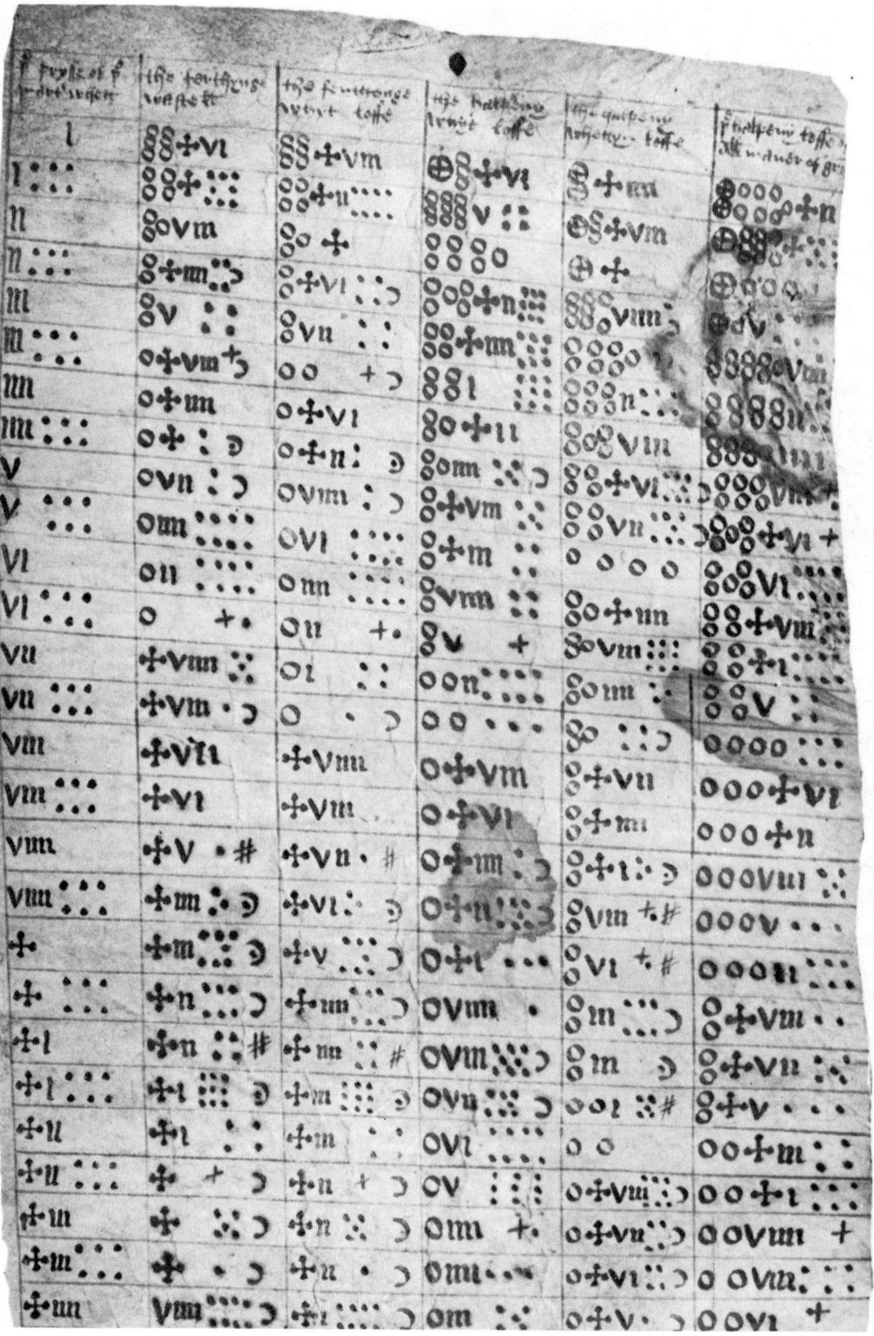

Fourteenth century fair-trading notice to be exhibited in the market. It shows the weights of farthing and ha'penny loaves varying according to the current price of corn.

The subcript matter reads:— 'Thys ys the sysse of all maner of bred of what corne or grayne so ever yt be yt shallbe wed (weighed) after the ferthynge wastell, for ye symnel (best wheaten loaf) shall wey less than ye wastell by 2s. because of ye sethynge (boiling), and ye ferthenge whytt loffe shall wey more than ye wastell by 2s. because of the brakinge (kneading), and ye halpeny whettyn loffe shall wey 3 ferthynge whytt lovys, and ye halpenny loffe of all maner of grayne shall wey 2 halpeny whytt lovys, and ye Baker shallbe alowed In every quarter of whete, for fornage (a sum due to a lord from a tenant for the right to bake in his own oven), 3d., for wod 3d., for 2 jornemen 3½d., for 2 pages (boys) (½d., for salte ½d., for barme ½d., for candyll ½d., and for his tydoge (watch-dog) ½d., & all hys Brane (bran), to hys avantage & thys ys the Statute of Wynchester. God Save the Kynge.'

perennial and uniquitous problems which face the consumer.

Shoppers in Andover's market often had other problems, some of which are recorded in the presentments made in the seventeenth century. In 1649 and 1650 part of the Market House—the part where the corn was sold—had been inclosed to the 'great preiudis to the Toune and Cuntry'. In 1652 the Hayward, John Peters was accused of, 'sufferin of hogs to Com into the market teareing of peoples sackes much to the predeudis of the cuntry'. In 1696 Thomas Mackrel, a wheelwright, was in trouble for 'laying of Weels and Laths in the street which is A greate Annoyence to the Inhabettants & the Market'; and the Bailiff was in trouble 'for not carrying the dunge to be caryed of the Market Place & the market house'. Perhaps today's market shoppers have less to cope with.

The market was probably in existence before the first charter establishing the Gild Merchant. The right to hold an annual Fair, and often the right to a weekly market was given by the King so that if any dispute arose over trading it could be settled by the King's Justices, and the King's Peace preserved. It would probably be during the Saxon period, that a time and place in Andover was set aside for the sale and purchase of perishable commodities. Buyers and sellers from the villages around would know when and where to come. As the market grew in size, it attracted merchants from other towns who by charter were allowed to trade outside their town without paying tax.

It was probably this freedom from paying tax that led the men of Andover to ask Henry II for a charter allowing them to trade as a Gild Merchant. It cost them ten marks of silver to regulate their own trade. New trades could now be introduced into the rural economy and more specialists recruited to raise the standard of life for the average person. In course of time, what had begun as a means of increasing the variety of merchandise sold became an excuse for selfishness, exclusivity and an obstacle to free trading. For instance in 1279, it was ordered that no fishmonger might have a stranger as a partner in anything offered for sale in the town under a penalty of 12d. In 1308 no stranger (from another town) has to buy 'fresh fish, capons, cocks, geese nor other fowls nor eggs before the first hour has struck'. For the first offence the fine was 12d., but a second offence meant the pillory.

The early records of the Gild Merchant which have been preserved do show some concern for fair trading. In 1262 a resolution was passed that no kersey cloths were to be made from Spanish wool, since the use of this wool instead of local wool damaged the reputation of Andover cloth. In 1272 there were at least nine merchants in Andover exporting wool to the weavers of Flanders. Alexander (the) Rich, was licensed to send 44 sacks, the others, Roger Chere, William de Golson, Thomas le Withe, Roger Shelde, Stephen Wolfel, Robert de Swyngere, John Spircock and John de Wymeldon, were licensed to send 20 sacks each. Not all this wool need have come from strictly local sources, but the amount is an indication of the strength and importance of Andover's Gild Merchant. Alexander Rich was also a royal official, having been appointed in 1270 to enquire into the goods of Flemish merchants and the debts owing to them. It was as a result of this interest in the wool trade that two Burgesses of Andover were summoned to meet the King at a 'parlement' in 1295 and for a few years, while trade was an important question in the national interest, Andover continued to send two burgesses, despite the expense.

The weekly market and the daily trade of the shopkeepers were the responsibility of the Gild Merchant but there were other necessaries which could not be supplied by Andover. For such goods, an annual fair was the feature to attract outsiders. An early grant of a fair was made in 1205 when King John authorised one on St Leonard's Day and the eve and morrow thereof, that is the 4th, 5th and 6th of November. Henry VIII granted another fair in 1511 to be held on the 1st, 2nd and 3rd of May. The 'Great Charter of 1599' lists four fairs which are granted to the Bailiff and Corporation of Andover. These are the two three-day fairs already noticed, another fair on Thursday and Friday of the Third Week in Lent, and 'one Fair to be holden yearly at Weyhill . . . together with a court of Pie Powder . . . and . . . Stallage, Picage, Fines, Amerciaments and all other Profits, Commodities and Emoluments whatsoever out of such Markets, Fairs and Court of Pie Powder . . .'

The Court of Pie Powder was not an extra source of income for the Bailiff; the Statute of Acton Burnell 1283 which established these courts named after the dusty feet of the merchants, intended them as a quick method of settling trading disputes. In fact it could involve wasting time over very little. More profitable for the Bailiff was the rent paid for the use of the hurdles within which the animals were penned, and the rent for the stall-places where not only traders but all sorts of entertainers could tempt the visitor to part with money.

It may be supposed that the Mid-Lent Fair was added by Queen Elizabeth, but the Weyhill Fair was far older than 1599. It is mentioned in the 'Vision of Piers Plowman' in 1365, and it probably grew up around a meeting of representatives of the villages of the

Out-Hundred of Andover assembled for their annual court or Law-day. Weyhill Fair was probably in existence before 1066, though the Bailiff's connection with it would start with the grant by King John in 1213 of the Out-Hundred of Andover. The effect of this was to make the Bailiffs and Stewards of Andover royal officers for the Michaelmas Law-day of the Out-Hundred held at Weyhill.

The Fair was held on some of the waste-land of Clanville or Ramridge Manor in Penton Grafton, and was convenient for all the villages in the Out-Hundred, being more or less central. As it was waste land, no rent was involved. Trouble arose when the men of Clanville came to an arrangement with Ewelme Hospital, the Lord of the Manor, to break up some new ground. In return for permission, they agreed to allow the Hospital and the Rector to enclose the waste of the manor, and these two then became owners of the land on which the fair had been held. Naturally, the farmer of these acres, as the tenant of Ewelme Hospital, and the Rector required some compensation for the disturbance caused by the erection of stalls and pens. Knowing that to remove the fair to some other waste land would be resented as a disturbance, the Corporation of Andover tried to obtain legal power to hold Weyhill Fair where they pleased. The series of lawsuits which had started in 1672 ended in 1694 when the Bailiff and Corporation were forced to rent the land for Weyhill Fair from Mr Drake, the farmer, and Dr Dixon, the Rector of Weyhill.

A map of Weyhill Fair illustrated with drawings of Ramridge House, Weyhill Church, a hare hunt, and other charming vignettes made in 1741 by William Burgess, shows the Fair Ground south of the present Weyhill Road and west of the Monxton road, while the stalls are on the north side of the Church. Fair time was a noisy, rowdy and exciting affair and frequently there were fires. In 1782 nine Justices of the Peace requested the Lord Chancellor to allow them to make a collection to relieve the sufferings of Thomas Pittard of Sherborne, a carrier, William New, of Andover, victualler, Sarah Sims of Fullerton, and James Barham of Stockbridge, victualler, in whose White Hart Booth, fire had broken out whence it spread quickly to other booths and standings and destroyed large quantities of hops and sundry goods to the value of £888-13-9.

The Rectory of Fyfield, Rev. Henry White, brother of Gilbert White of Selborne, in his diary for 12 October 1782 recorded 'Hop Fair mostly finished very few brt. and almost all sold, the best at £10 and £11 old and bad abt. £6 per cwt. Selborne sd to have sent their whole crop in one Waggon!' Perhaps the fire was a fortunate occurrence after all. On 11 October 1783 he recorded 'Hops, none from Selborne, and very few from that district; few from Farnham, and a very thin shew on the Hill. tho some Kentish and some old hops were bot. Best price £11 per cwt. Bought none. Weyhill being the worst market when they are dear, the best when they are cheap.'

The Weyhill Fair, in 1744 'reckoned one of the biggest in England for Hops, Cheese, and several other Commodities and for sheep there is none so big' was already declining in importance when William Cobbett saw it in the 1830s. It lasted as a general fair until 1914, and was renewed as a Sheep Auction annually for one day until 1957. Auctions announced for 1958 and 1959 were cancelled because not enough sheep were being offered for sale. The other three fairs which were held in Andover, Mid-Lent, May and St Leonard's were much less important and more of a nuisance to the inhabitants. At the Mid-Lent Fair, cheese, earthenware, cloth and brooms were sold; at the other two, cheese, hops, rakes, and for all three the 'usual standings' were available. A list of these standings made in the early seventeenth century has been preserved. There were standings for 56 shoemakers, 5 trunkmen, 41 hatters, 6 smiths, 1 ironmonger, 13 sackmen, and 8 other traders in North Row and South Row. In London Street were 3 collarmakers, 3 leatherclothes sellers, 1 cutler, 2 saddlers and 1 mercer and 41 other standings. In Cross Row, a further 16 standings, and in 'The Booths' 19 glovers, 3 braziers, 1 barber, 2 bottlemakers and 7 butchers, brings the total to 261 standings altogether.

The decline of the Fair was due to changes in transport which made it possible to buy commodities as and when they were needed. Turnpike roads, canals, and railways rendered stocking up for a whole year unnecessary, and small shops began to appear in villages about 1830. After an appeal by the townsfolk to the Town Council in 1869, it was unanimously decided on 5 February 1870 that 'these fairs produce more injury than benefit to the Town generally, and are become a positive menace'. Taking advice from the Town Clerk of Basingstoke, where the Michaelmas Fair had been discontinued since 1868, Andover Town Council proceeded to take the necessary steps to discontinue the Town Fairs, keeping only the St Leonard's Sheep Fair, and the newly instituted Wool Fair. Even the latter left the Corporation's control in 1887, when it was amalgamated with an auction held by F. C. Ellen. In that year, the Sheep Fair in November produced a balance of £44-14-11 (receipts £70-0-3 and expenses £25-5-4).

One essential item of both Fairs and Markets was an accurate set of weights and measures. Normally kept in Andover, they had to be carried to and from Weyhill as numerous receipts and bills testify. A complete set of the dry measures rested for many years on a bookcase in the Public Library. These and a set of weights and a scale caused many intriguing entries in the Council Minute Books, and in the collection of vouchers.

W. H. W. Titheridge, an Inspector of Weights and Measures charged 6/1 in December 1835 for adjusting and stamping weights and measures. In the mid nineteenth century, the post of Inspector of Weights and Measures was held by the Superintendent of Police in Andover until 1878 when it was assumed by the Borough Surveyor, who under the Weights and Measures Act adjusted and stamped these at the Guildhall between 10 and 12 noon on the First Monday and Tuesday in March, June, September and December.

Another essential item for the Market was the Market Bell. Its sound began and ended trading for the day. The Market Bell depended in turn upon the Market Clock, and this piece of mechanism caused a great deal of expense. Every few years it had to be repaired and regulated, and there was also the daily duty of winding up the weights for which the Sexton was paid an annual fee of two guineas after 1789.

To make sure that the Market Clock was visible it was gilded. In 1744 the cost of gilding the vane, scrolls, cupola, crown, large and small balls of the Clockface came to £6-10-0. It was cheaper to mend the iron gates to the Market House; a mere 6/- in 1809. Nine guineas was the cost of making steps around the Market House which had been built in 1726 at a cost of about £300; the receipted bills for the various items, lime, sand, bricks, wood, glass, lead, tiles, and so forth are still in the collection of bills and vouchers which form part of the Archives.

The Market House has also been called the Town Hall, the Corn Exchange, and since 1920 the Guildhall. When built in 1825 the lower floor was open on all sides, and there was a staircase leading up to the Council Chamber and the Assembly Room on the first floor. As the amount of trade increased, the stalls spread out on to the area south of the Hall. Paved in 1855 at the same time as the lower floor was enclosed this area sufficed for many years. When the Cenotaph was erected in 1920 in place of the Golden Jubilee drinking fountain and lampstandard—now sadly relegated to the Council depot—it became a little incongruous among the rapidly increasing numbers of stalls. The increase was gradual but by 1939 the whole of the centre of the Lower High Street was taken up by stallholders of the market.

The charges for these stalls increased with time, so it is very pleasant to read in the Borough Council Minutes of the consideration with which the members treated the handicapped. On 2 October 1886 the Council resolved that Mr Stevens 'who had for many years only paid 6d for a stand at the rails near the Market House should, in consideration of his being a cripple, be allowed to keep it there without any increased charge'.

Fair trading was the reason for the creation of the Gild Merchant. For many years the Gild fulfilled its duty by preventing unfair practices, but, as its numbers grew so did its inability to carry out its primary function. But one Gild was still too big in the days of Queen Elizabeth. With the advice of the Earl of Leicester, High Steward of Andover in 1575, the Gild was divided into three Companies or Brotherhoods. The Leathermen's Company naturally included anyone connected with leather, saddlers, glovers, shoemakers, collarmakers, butchers and undertakers; the Drapers' Company included those concerned with cloth, fullers, weavers, tailors, hosiers as well as fletchers, coopers and fishmongers; the Haberdashers' Company included milliners and mercers, cappers and hatmakers and brewers, bakers, vintners and innholders.

The original members of these companies were those already practising in Andover, who had only to register their names for a licence to trade. Newcomers had to pay £5 if a native, and £6-8-4 if an alien, for permission to open a shop and trade within the limits of the town. By 1800 this practice had almost ceased; increased trade and movement made it impossible to keep track of everyone.

The last minute in the Haberdashers' Company Book on Monday 17 March 1807 indicates a rethinking of the position which resulted in total abandonment. Free trade had come to Andover sooner than it did to the Nation.

Free trade, fair trade and false trade, Andover has seen all three many times. Though the Wool market which brought the Bradford merchants to Andover has gone, though the Weyhill Fair which supplied many breweries with essential ingredients and the Rector of Fyfield with half a year's supply of cheese has vanished, though the Corn Exchange which once filled the lower floor of the Guildhall is forgotten, that same area is still used on Friday mornings for the Women's Institute Market, and sometimes on Saturdays for jumble sales. And below the steadily moving hands of the Market Clock, though no one takes any great notice of it today when everyone has a wristwatch, the market traders every Saturday morning sell to the general public in the Market Place.

Chapter Six
THE GUILDHALL

'Who calls the council, states the certain day,
Who forms the phalanx and who points the way?'

Standing at the northern end of the market place is that classically proportioned building known since 1920, when Edmund Parsons persuaded the Town Council to rename it, as the Guildhall. The name marks the antiquity of Andover's self government, shared with a few other Hampshire towns, about which many thousands of words have already been written elsewhere. The Guild was the Gild Merchant incorporated by the Charter of Henry II in 1175, confirmed by the Charters of Richard I in 1194 and of John in 1205. The last of these documents, the only one to survive is the oldest dated document belonging to Andover, and as such is the most often seen and the most well known.

Another charter dated 31 October 1213 granted to the men of Andover, 'the manor of Andover with the Out Hundred for a rent of £80 blanched for the ancient farm and £20 by number for the increase'. The rent of Andover, that is the sums of money due to the Lord of the Manor were commuted to two payments, 40 lbs of silver and £10 in silver pennies at Easter, and again at Michaelmas. The rents would have been collected by the Sheriff of Hampshire, but by this charter, the money was to be paid direct to the King's Treasury. Two further charters dated 6 July 1265, were granted by Henry III from Clarendon near Salisbury. One of these granted to the men of Andover that their goods would not be seized for debts for which they had not stood bail, unless they were the principal debtors, that their goods would not be confiscated if they died without making a will and that their dogs need not have any toes removed unless they lived in the forest. (Forest dwelling dogs needed artificially slowing down, for the benefit of the deer.) The other charter granted to the men of Andover that all royal letters concerning the Town and Out-Hundred of Andover should be addressed to them and not to the Sheriff of Hampshire.

By virtue of these charters, the men of Andover, and their families, became a self governing community, independent of the Sheriff of the county. Independence was not total, for the Sheriff collected the profits of the Priory during the war with France. Naturally there were disputes between the Gild Merchant and the Sheriff as to the limits of his authority, as an entry in the Gild Rolls for 1345 shows. On this occasion 'Edware atte Morische was fined 20s. because he caused a delivery of cattle to be made in accordance with a writ of the Sheriff to the prejudice of the community and contrary to the liberties of the town'.

Some of the records of the Gild Merchant have been preserved. One group of rolls which begin with the year 1262 and continue with breaks to 1346 are known as the Morespech—or Morrowspeech— for the meetings were held in the mornings usually on Fridays. A second group recording details of meetings between 1489 and 1574 (with breaks) are known as 'maneloquia'. The change from 'morrowspeech' to 'maneloquia' occurs in 1454 and may be connected with a feeling that an English word was an unsuitable start to a Latin entry. Andover was becoming conscious of its civic dignity. Growth was slow but fortunately free from conflict with competing authorities like sheriffs, earls, bishops or abbots.

Most of the business recorded on these rolls concerns the protection of existing traders and the prevention of trading abuses. There are occasional hints of a wider field than trade. In 1301 it was decreed that the death of a man should be signalled by ringing the 'great bell', and that 'no man's beast shall enter the churchyard or graze there and that if the priest or vicar wishes to have the grass he shall cut it and carry it away'. The Gild Merchant itself had no legal function but it had acquired through its charters the right to collect a heriot—the mediaeval version of estate duty, usually the best horse or cow, or some other item of value—for the succession. As tenants of the King, the Gild had to supply armed men for service and an item in 1328 records the purchase of seven sets of armour, headpiece, doublet, and gloves, which were expected to be well used in the Hundred Years War which was just starting.

The Gild Merchant not only charged for admission to its ranks, but expelled and refused admission if necessary. In 1316, Robert Horn had his privileges taken away from him because 'he laid hands on Thomas the Bowyere, the Sergeant At Mace and reviled the fraternity'. In 1327, the Gild refused admission to Roger le Beyr because he was a 'born bondsman of Thomas Spircock, Lord of Upper Clatford', and as such could not be allowed to trade with the free men of Andover.

The admission fee was 60/-, and the Gild Merchant also received money from the fines which were imposed upon those whose trading practices were frowned upon. In 1328, the Gild decided that it would charge a fee for enrolling any transfer of property, 12d if the property was worth more than £10, and 6d if less. As the revenue of the Gild increased above the amount or rent—or fee-farm—which was due to the King or his nominee, the surplus was invested in land.

Before the Gild Merchant came to an end in 1575, it had acquired a Gildhall in the new market place. The weekly market was held in the open space on the ground floor, while in the closed chamber above the Bailiffs and Steward would hold their Courts, and the Twenty Four Forwardmen to whom the Gild had entrusted the running of Andover in 1415, could hold their meetings.

From an early period the Gild had elected two Bailiffs who as the leading citizens witnessed conveyances of land. The electoral arrangement after 1415 was that the Forwardmen would choose two more names to add to the two left over from the previous year, and from these four names, the Seneschall and the two Bailiffs would, at a meeting on the Sunday nearest Michaelmas choose the next pair of Bailiffs.

Occasionally, the Gild or the Twenty Four would need legal advice and then it was useful to have someone close to the King to help them. The office of Steward of Andover was held in 1387 by Sir John Sands, between 1401 and 1406 possibly by Sir Thomas Skelton, and in 1424 by Sir Walter Saundes. A deed of appointment survives from 1544 when Richard Rawlyns and Thomas Lake, Bailiffs of Andover 'by the assent consent and agreement of ower brethryn and off the holle Corporation of the sayde Towne . . . gyve and graunt to the worshipfull Sir Thomas Wrythowsley Knight one of the two principall secretaries of the King's Highness' the office of Steward for the terme of his lyfe naturall'.

In 1584 the Earl of Leicester, who was High Steward of Andover, wanted more support in the newly called Parliament for his policy of military intervention in Holland. Thinking that Andover elected two representatives, he wrote to the Bailiff asking to nominate one or both of the members, freeing the town from the burden (2/- per day) of maintaining these men at Westminster. The Bailiff had to tell him that Andover sent no Members to Parliament, and the Earl persuaded the Queen to summon two Burgesses from her loyal Town of Andover to her next Parliament in 1586. Andover was the last town to be added to the list of Boroughs.

The Earl of Leicester appears to have been disregarded the year before. On 25 January 1583 the Forwardmen agreed with Lord de la Warr, Sir William Kingsmill and Mr Thornbrough for a new Guildhall. The agreement sets out the conditions of the building in which it appears that it would be a free gift to the town, for one condition of the agreement was that no repayment of any money or any other contribution was envisaged. This explains why the Twenty Four accepted the major condition which was that only half of the lower floor of the Guildhall should be partitioned into shops or stalls for the Approved Men of the Corporation, while the other half of the floor should be a common market available to all. Perhaps the gentlemen were acting for the Earl of Leicester, or that as three local, public spirited and wealthy men they had combined to find space for country folk to sell in the market house, where most of the space had been pre-empted by the Forwardmen (i.e. Approved Men) for their own use.

The Earl of Essex was High Steward of Andover at the time of the 'Great Charter of 1599' but appears to have done little to help. John Moore of North Baddesley was the Town's Steward and he was paid extra for his 'paynes in our towne buisness'. The reason for the Charter was that the piecemeal way in which the town's privileges had been granted in the past had led to 'divers Disputes Questions and Ambiguities'. For example, could land on a tenancy be inherited under the terms of a will?

The 'Great Charter' which remained effective until 1835, contained detailed regulations for the establishment of a Corporation of Approved Men (11 named) and Capital Burgesses (12 named) and a Steward (John Moore). One of the Approved Men, subject to the Steward's veto, was to be Bailiff, Coroner, Escheator, Clerk of the Market and Justice, for one year from Michaelmas, while two other Approved Men were to be Justices; all to be chosen on the Monday before the feast of Holy Cross—that is between 7 and 13 September.

The business of the Corporation did not change much after 1599, though it increased in scope in the eighteenth century. The Corporation leased arable lands in the Town fields, and the other Town and Charity properties. It concerned itself with the proper conduct of its members, levying fines for non attendance, and excluding them when guilty of insulting behaviour. It also dealt with the mastership of the Free Grammar School, and the maintenance of its buildings. It tried to insist on the proper accounting of the Town's money, and, not always successfully, with the money given for 'Charitable Uses'. It elected two members of

Parliament when requested, and it negotiated loans and mortgages, but there was no real attempt to improve the conditions of life in Andover. In 1621, the Corporation did propose to fine inhabitants who did not 'repair, make, maintain and amend the Pitching or Pavement of the Street . . . from his house to the Channel in every place where the same shall be decayed, within six weeks after warning'. Four years later, they ordered that when this work was being done, and for ten days afterwards, no one should drive any cart through the streets that were being repaired—a necessary precuation in a chalky area. In 1663, the Corporation appointed a Common Carrier, and proposed to fine anyone else £20 for carrying any goods from Andover.

A real crisis came in 1692. At that time, the Corporation was involved in the lawsuits over Weyhill Fair, and a rumour spread that part of the 'Charitable Uses' funds were being used to pay the legal costs. The Bailiff on 29 July 'ordered that a due & speedy inspection be hadd of all the accts belonging to the Charitable uses and that all Guifts Donattions & Accts thereto be fully taken and fairely writt', so that 'all persons may be satisfyed how that affair stands that the town and publique Officers may be freed of the scandall throwne upon them by ill men'. A fortnight later, 'It is this day ordered that an Inspection be made into all the Charities of this towne and that Notice be tymely & publeqly given to all persons that wee will meet this day sennight to heare all complaynts & receyve any informacons of any miscarriages in or about the said Charities'.

Before the week was up, however, one irate inhabitant, William Hayward or Howard had fixed two copies of a paper, one to the West Door of the Church, the other on the door of the Independent Chapel in Soper's Lane, on which he listed the lands and rents which were paid to the Corporation and those which should have been devoted to the relief of the poor. He was immediately hauled before the Corporation and punished for his 'aspertions' and 'misdemeanours' by being whipped from the Gaol to the Upper Angel without benefit of appeal. Within six weeks, the Corporation had placed a wooden board in the Church on which they listed all the benefactions which had been made to the Corporation of Andover. The haste with which this 'Benefactions Tablet' was made accounts for the numerous mistakes in its statements. The sharpness of the Corporation's reaction suggests a cover up. Perhaps William Hayward's allegations were not unfounded, and they were afraid that defalcations would come to light.

There were minor crises in Andover's Corporation, just as there were political crises on the national scale during the period of the later Stuarts. In 1679 there was a dispute over the election of a Bailiff. Of the twenty two men present, eleven including the presiding Bailiff wanted William Barwicke while the others wanted Thomas Westcombe. The dispute was taken by petition to the Privy Council, which met at Whitehall in November to hear the evidence. When it was revealed that two new members of the Corporation had promised to vote for Barwicke before they were elected to the ranks of the oligarchy, the Privy Council cancelled the result and declared the post forfeit to Thomas Westcombe. The two corrupted members of the Corporation were duly expelled.

A brief connection with the East India Company was the cause of another political scandal. The two Members elected by the Corporation were both supporters of the East India Company, and their opponents proved that Samuel Shepheard M.P. for Newport I.O.W. had been guilty of bribery in five constituencies including Andover, for which his son Francis had been elected. The Bailiff of Andover, Julius Samborne, and the two Justices, Joseph Wimbleton and Edward Warham were taken into custody by the Sergeant-at-Arms, imprisoned in the Tower, brought to the Bar of the House, forced to beg for pardon on their knees, and severely reprimanded before being released.

There was a similar confusion after the death of Queen Anne in 1714. The general attitude of the Corporation was Whig rather than Tory, but Cornelius Tirrell persuaded the Steward, William Guidott, to appoint him as his Deputy and Town Clerk on 9 April 1715, when the position of the Jacobites and the Hanoverians was still in the balance. He proceeded to fill the vacancies in the Corporation with Tories—but not for long. On 9 July 1715, Richard Widmore came to the Corporation with a document from William Guidott revoking Tirrell's appointment and his own deputation as Town Clerk. Tirrell took action in the King's Bench Court, but lost.

More important, however, was the condition of the Guildhall which needed increased expenditure on repairs as it grew older. The decision to pull down the old and build a new was finally taken in 1724. Typical of its period, the new Guildhall was an early Georgian building in brick and Chilmark stone with arches and pillars of the Corinthian order. The surveyor, or Clerk of the Works, was Stephen Switzur from East Stratton near Micheldever.

Information about the work of the Corporation in the eighteenth century is more complete because the Minute Books from this period have survived. How much of the content of the meeting is recorded

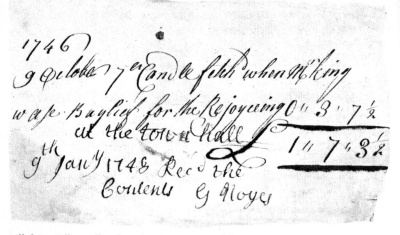

Bill for a 7 lb candle when the Corporation celebrated the news of Culloden, 1746; receipted over two years later.

depended upon the character of the Town Clerk. One meeting seems to have transacted no business at all. A new broom could galvanise the Corporation into actions not hitherto contemplated. Before 1752 the business of leases and elections was varied by apprenticing nine boys to local tradesmen, negotiating a loan with the Earl of Portsmouth which he graciously converted into a free gift, and a quarrel over the use of the Corporation's pew in the Church. In 1752, there was an avalanche of activity following the appointment of a new Town Clerk, Ralph Etwall. Encroachments were pounced upon and punished; vacancies in the Corporation were tracked down and filled; a lecturer was appointed under the terms of Richard Kemis' will to preach in the afternoon of the last Sunday of each month; new arrangements were made for the 'Aldermen's Feast', namely, thirty shillings for an ordinary dinner for the Bailiff, Corporation, Town Clerk, Minister, Schoolmaster, Sergeant-at-Mace and other officers: a one-guinea limit was fixed for a drink on the King's Birthday, Coronation Day, and Prince of Wales' Birthday, and the other anniversaries; and a new book of oaths was ordered, the old one 'being worn and almost unintelligible'. The old book was carefully preserved although it was no longer needed.

Within a few years the Corporation was engaging in public works like Turnpike Roads and a Pest House, ordering the Bailiff to 'Fish in the River as usual', appointing a Gamekeeper for the Manor and Hundred, opposing a County Workhouse, settling a dispute over water-meadows, and desiring Sir John Griffin Griffin, K.B., M.P. 'to use his vote to obtain a total stop of exportation of all sorts of corn'.

Not all the activity was productive. On one occasion at least the Corporation may have tried to use their power to elect to an unpopular office as a punitive measure. Robert Stanford was ordered to quit Corporation's property at Michaelmas 1768. For some reason, but possibly a remark which he made, the Corporation proceeded to elect him as Constable in his absence and to impose a penalty of £20 if he did not swear the oath within ten days. Stanford refused to serve as Constable. The Corporation sought their Steward's opinion, and then Sir Fletcher Norton's opinion, and as a result prosecuted Stanford at the July Assizes. A mistake in the indictment allowed Stanford to pay a fine of £8 to be relieved of his duty. As the Town Clerk's bill for legal expenses was already £109-4-1, at least this token sum was more acceptable than a doubled bill for a second prosecution.

The Minutes of the Corporation include both national and local events. On 6 November 1775 the Corporation agreed that 'a Dutiful and loyal address be presented to his majesty on the present posture of public affairs'. Rawlins Hillman, who had been elected Approved Man in August 1775 was not able to attend a meeting to take the oath until 1779, because he was 'absent in america'. He was elected a second time, to make sure. At the same time the Corporation was aware of local possibilities. On Wednesday 18 April 1770, they enjoined the Bailiff and Justices to be 'vigilant and use their utmost endeavours to prevent bonfires Fireworks mobs and riots in the Borough this evening'. It is the only evidence for any Hocktide revelry in Andover.

The Guildhall was a constant source of concern. In 1788, £242 needed to be spent on it. Then in 1820 an estimate for repairs came to £431-3-0, which was deferred for further consideration when it was brought to the Corporation's notice in September as 'the season being too far advanced', or because they could then see no way of financing the repairs. Four years later the financial prospects were brighter and in May 1824 a new survey of the Town Hall was ordered. Thereafter events moved faster; perhaps it was really necessary, though the building was barely 100 years old. In July 1824, the Corporation considered plans for rebuilding, preserving the form of the 'present front'. In January 1825, the Town Clerk presented the Report of the Committee on the new Guildhall; the plans of John Harris Langdon had been approved and estimates for its construction in Bath stone had been submitted; William Gibbs,

£1600 for the stonework, William Lansley £1260 for the carpenters' work, Joseph Turner £355-17-0 for the bricklayers' work, John Windover £57-10-0 for slating, Robert Tasker £114-18-0 for ironwork, William Herberts, for plumbing and glazing, and Mr Beare for painting; gifts of £1,000 each from the two Members, Thomas Assheton Smith M.P. and Sir John Pollen, M.P. should be accepted, as should a loan of £2,000 at 5% from Robert Sutton of London. The Corporation agreed to this report, appointed Langdon as Surveyor and Architect, asked him to proceed with expedition, designated the large front room at the Angel as the Guildhall, and ordered the Council Chest containing all the charters to be deposited in George Barnes' room.

It appears that almost all the vouchers, receipts and certificates of work done have been preserved. Among them are receipted bills for events on 3 May 1826. Two guineas was paid to Rob. Cherry for ringing the bells; £16-4-0 was paid to John Woodward, landlord of the Star, for twelve one-guinea dinners for the Rt. Hon the Earl of Portsmouth, Sir John Pollen, M.P., Thomas A. Smith, M.P., Rev. Robert Cole, Schoolmaster, Rev. William Pedder, Curate of Andover, J. H. Langdon and 2 friends, and Messrs. Williams, Harrington, Turner, and Wheeler, together with 6 bottles of sherry and 5 of port; £7-14-0 to John Evans, landlord of the Bush, for 36 dinners at 2/- each and 36 gallons of beer at 2/- a gallon; and £13-6-0 to Robert Maud for 174 gallons of beer and the cost of 'repairing casks broken by the Populace'. The foundation stone was well and truly laid, but despite all the celebrations, when it was completed the chimneys smoked.

On 8 June 1826, the Corporation moved into the new Council Chamber in the new Guildhall. Furnishing it needed another £600,

Cartoon on the Municipal Stakes, Andover, 1880. The result was Edward Reynolds (Mayor) 473 votes, John Moore 420 votes, F. Ellen 419 votes, J. H. Stagg 326 votes,

and in such splendid surroundings the Corporation might have moved at its accustomed leisurely pace, if the tempo of national events had not forced them to change. In October 1830, Mr. Mann, a local solicitor who was not a member of the Corporation, protested against the illegality of the elections, and forced the Town Clerk to obtain a writ of Mandamus so that elections for the Bailiff and Justices had to be held a second time. The Corporation then became aware that many of their number were merely sleeping members, and began a clearing out process with letters of resignation and elections to vacancies. It was in vain. The final meeting of the old Corporation was held on 7 September 1835 but no Bailiff or Justices were elected to serve for the next year.

Instead an elected Borough Council met on 31 December 1835 to choose four new Aldermen and on the following day, to appoint Robert Dowling the first Mayor of Andover; Harry Footner continued as Town Clerk. Among their first tasks were to decide on a suitable salary for the Town Clerk, to appoint a Treasurer, a Recorder, a Finance Committee and a Watch Committee, and to fix the dates of their Quarterly Meetings. The minutes of these early meetings include transcripts of letters to Lord John Russell, Home Secretary, and An Address to His Majesty thanking him for 'the blessings we enjoy under your Majesty's mild and paternal government'.

Andover has indeed been fortunate in its executive officer, the Town Clerk. The Old Corporation was served by Ralph Etwall (1752–88) and his son Ralph Etwall (1788–1813), by Richard Footner (1813–33) and his son Harry Footner (1833–75), who combined the part time post of Town Clerk with a private practice. The rising flood of Public Health legislation made it more difficult for Richard

10 to 1 on THE STAG   *30 to 1 on EASTFIELD*   *20 to 1 on HONEY BOX*   *THE MARE WINS*

Geo. Kossuth Reynolds 314 votes, P. Pontings 234 votes, L. Cole 179 votes, G. J. R. Goodden 55 votes.

Footner (1875–85) and T. E. Longman (1885–1930). C. J. Phillips (1930–38) became the first full-time Town Clerk and was followed by E. J. O. Gardiner, LL.B. (1938–51) who went on to work for the Association of Municipal Corporations and J. F. Garner, LL.M. (1951–60) who later became Professor of Law at Nottingham. The last Town Clerk, John Whatley, LL.B. (1960–74) brings the total to ten Town Clerks in over two centuries, and this gave Andover a firm executive basis on which to operate.

Between 1835 and 1875 the Borough Council was only one of a number of authorities with conflicting duties and responsibilities. Beyond the control of the Council was the Vestry, or Parish Council, which under the Vicar and Churchwardens was responsible for the upkeep of the Church, the Churchyard, and the fire precautions. They also appointed Surveyors of the Highways and Overseers of the Poor, whose main duty after the establishment of the Poor Law Union in 1835 was to collect the rates, both for the Union, and for the Borough whenever authorised. The roads within three quarters of a mile of the Guildhall were the responsibility of the Paving Commissioners, a large body of prominent citizens including many of the Council. Since any seven could act for all, the elected councillors could act as Paving Commissioners in such matters as paving, lighting, draining and policing the streets though the Borough Council was also the Watch Committee by virtue of another Act. The major roads into Andover were cared for by two Turnpike Trusts. The Board of Guardians who had taken over the care of the poor and the sick were responsible to the Poor Law Commissioners in London.

Excluded from these areas of responsibility by other statutory bodies, the new Borough Council could function only in a limited way. Furthermore, they had inherited a considerable debt, and in the new circumstances could enter only into such financial transactions as were approved by the Treasury. The arrangement caused delays and uncertainties, particularly over the sale of corporate property. Often a sale made at one valuation had to be set aside because the Treasury had re-valued it. Nevertheless, by 1867 the monstrous debt of £3,000 had been liquidated by the sale of most of the property inherited from the old Corporation.

The new Municipal Council was a body with a limited vision. On 1 February 1868 the Councillors decided not to collect a local subscription for the victims of the Clerkenwell Explosion, but in May 1876 they decided on a congratulatory address on the return of the Prince of Wales from India. On 5 February 1870, the Council refused to subscribe to the British Association on the Treatment and Utilization of Sewage, but in July 1879 ordered a letter of condolence to the Empress Eugenie on the untimely death of the Prince Imperial. In November 1877 the Council refused to subscribe to the Shakespeare Memorial Theatre at Stratford, but on 3 February 1878 they did ask their local M.P., Lt. Col Wellesley to support the second reading of the Manchester Corporation Water Bill.

The Municipal Council was forced to adopt other functions slowly. First the Burials Act 1865 enforced the formation of a Burials Board to take over the care and management of the Churchyard from the Vestry. Then in 1866, the Cattle Plague Prevention Act forced them to form a Committee and appoint a Cattle Plague Inspector, for which post they chose R. Gates, a Veterinary Surgeon in Bridge Street, and he became Inspector under the Contagious Diseases (Animals) Act 1869 when that came into force.

In April 1871, the Council felt itself sufficiently important to have its arms emblazoned on a flag and sent for display to the forthcoming International Exhibition, though when the Supervisor of Excise called for the duty on the use of armorial bearings, the Council defended its refusal by claiming that the 'Great Charter of 1599' enforced the use of arms on its seal. It was because the Mayor, Alderman Gue, found himself without a badge of office when he attended the International Exhibition with fellow Mayors, that he procured a Chain and Badge which he offered to the Council. Naturally it was accepted, and at the next meeting the Council re-elected him as Mayor and presented him with a copy of his offer inscribed on 'illuminated vellum'. This was the William Gue who years previously, in search of employment, had walked from Romsey in shoes which were not a pair. Gue's chain was stolen from the Council Offices at Beech Hurst one night in 1960 and now reposes at the bottom of the Brentford lock of the Grand Union Canal where it was thrown by the thief.

The Public Health Act 1872 created more work. The Town Clerk became Clerk to the Urban Sanitary Authority, and William Marsh was appointed Inspector of Nuisances (at £40 p.a.) and the Treasurer's salary increased from £15 to £30 p.a. The Council, however, were reluctant to appoint a Medical Officer of Health and despite pressure from the Local Government Board waited until June 1874, when the Medical Officer to the Board of Guardians, Dr Septimus B. Farr agreed to serve on a fee-paid basis. Later in 1874, William Marsh was appointed Surveyor in place of the Surveyors of the Highways. As an Andover Volunteer Fire Brigade had been formed in 1867, and as Overseers of the Poor were now appointed by the Council, the Vestry became unimportant

The Council sat as an Urban Sanitary Authority for the first time in 1875; because of the increased business, the Council now had to meet monthly at 10 a.m. on the first Saturday of the month. The Minutes record many interesting sidelights on human values, as for example on 4 March 1899 when the Council refused to support the Local Government Officers Superannuation Bill on the grounds that these officers were part-timers. When the Town Clerk requested a 'Papyrograph' in May 1877 to help him in reproducing the reports and other memoranda which the increased work made necessary, the Council decided to let the question stand over. On the other hand, the idea of saving a little money annually by purchasing a horse instead of hiring one seemed good. The horse which was purchased from Mr Ivy Hedderley in January 1876 cost £44 but the stabling for horse, harness, carts and so on was very costly. Another horse was purchased in 1888 and pensioned off in June 1900.

Among the minor affairs which occupied the Town Council was the problem of the bandstand. In July 1900 the Andover Town Band and the Temperance Band requested permission to use the bandstand in the Recreation Ground on Sundays and Wednesdays. The Council finally decided to allow the Town Band to play on Sundays from 8 p.m. to 9 p.m. while the Temperance Band played from 3 p.m. to 5 p.m. and on Wednesdays the Town Band alternated with the Temperance Band from 5 p.m. to 9 p.m. during the summer.

For many years an annual letter was received, often from Miss Becker, Secretary to the Manchester National Society for Women's Suffrage, asking for the Council's support for a petition to remove the electoral disabilities of women. Naturally the Council let these letters lie on the table. Yet though women in general may not have been worthy of support, the Queen's Diamond Jubilee was celebrated by a vast feast in the High Street. A footnote to the Minutes for 6 May 1876 records that 'After the Quarterly Meeting of the Council this day held, the Mayor, T. P. Clarke Esqre proceeded, with the Mace Bearers and Town Clerk to the central window of the Guildhall and from thence proclaimed Her Most Gracious Majesty as 'Empress of India' in addition to her royal titles'.

Within a century, both the Empire and the Borough Council had disappeared. The structure of local government appropriate for the Victorian era was considered with some justification to be inadequate to meet the needs of the late twentieth century. As part of a national reorganisation, Andover Borough Council combined with

Andover Rural District and Romsey & Stockbridge Rural District Councils into a Test Valley District Council. The inaugural meeting of the new authority was held in the Guildhall at Andover on Thursday 21 June 1973, nine months before the take-over date. Among all the the good wishes for a long, glorious and happy career for the new Council, and the expressions of pride, humility and gratitude from individuals, was the crucial statement 'We must bury the old anachronism of town and country and get rid of the antipathy which has sometimes existed between countryman and townsman. We have to build a very new and special relationship between the three communities'. Thus ended the endeavours of the townsfolk of Andover to manage the business of their town without reference to the inhabitants of the surrounding rural areas, and independent of national and county authorities until the final hundred years.

From the granting of the first charter by Henry II in 1175 until 1974 the affairs of the Town had been conducted, in the main, by successive generations of merchants and shopkeepers, aided at one time by some of the landed gentry, and in later years by members of the professional classes. For much of the time it was a struggle to maintain the dignity of a Borough against a background of meagre civic resources and innate financial caution.

When the Test Valley District Council was created, the place of the Borough Council as the symbol of the people of Andover was taken by the Charter Trustees. These were the elected District Councillors from the four, and later five, wards of Andover, with very limited powers but with the responsibility of ensuring the continuity of Andover's heritage. This body ceased to exist when the Test Valley was granted Borough status in December 1976, but the identity of Andover will continue to reside in the civic pride of its inhabitants as much as in its Guildhall.

Chapter Seven
THE COURTHOUSE

'All crimes shall cease, and ancient fraud shall fail
Returning Justice lift aloft her scale;'

For several hundred years, the Guildhall functioned as the Courthouse for Andover. The only other indication of Andover's legal tradition of seven centuries is the series of court rolls dating from as far back as 1272. The fact that a roll has survived for 700 years is no indication of the importance of its contents which are frequently trivial or else so brief as to be a mere record of the names of the parties involved. Typical of the more interesting cases is a complaint by Emma le Archer of Charlton in 1283 that, on Monday after Hockday between 3 p.m. and 6 p.m. an ox broke through her fence from the field belonging to Roger Pynniger, to which Roger replied that it was Emma's fault for not keeping her fences in good condition. In the next roll Thomas Godlake accused Hugh Cupping of assaulting him by force and unjustly maltreating him, slandering him, calling him a malingerer, and accusing him of being a night-prowler for which he claimed damages of 5/-. Similar neighbourly disputes occur, no doubt, in every generation, though they may not be brought to the Courts of the In-Hundred and Out-Hundred.

These courts were granted to his 'Men of Andover' by King John in his charter of 1213, and the presiding officer at the courts was the Bailiff of Andover. The courts were held every Monday alternately for the In-Hundred and the Out-Hundred. The In-Hundred consisted of the tythings of Charlton, Hatherden, Enham Regis, Alderman-le-Grand—the area around and including the Upper High Street, Priory—the area around the Church, and Winchester Street, which also included the lower High Street and Bridge Street.

Similarly, tythingmen came to the Court of the Out-Hundred from the parishes of Abbotts Ann, Amport, Cholderton and Appleshaw, Upper Clatford, Fyfield, Grately, Kimpton and Littleton, Knights Enham, Penton Mewsey, Thruxton, South Tidworth and Penton Grafton. The chief interest to be derived from the early rolls of civil cases is that they show the beginnings of surnames. Some of these distinguishing names indicate a trade, Thomas le Carter, Emma le Archer, Richard le Copare, Thomas le Barchir (a barker associated with tanning) and William le Marchal (generally the blacksmith). Sometimes nicknames are used; Alexander le Riche, Robert le Dun (with brown hair or beard), Thomas le Red (later Read). Names sometimes derive from places: John de Marisco (Marsh), Peter att Mill, Richard de Bradefield are examples.

The earliest record of a Court for views of Frankpledge is 1379, but the system was started in the reign of King Edgar. It was essentially a practical method of maintaining law and order by making neighbours responsible for each other's good behaviour. Neighbours were grouped into tythings, and each member of the tything could be held responsible for the damage caused by a fellow member. One man from each tything—the tythingman—had to report any crime at the View of Frankpledge held in the Hundred. The View was usually held by the Sheriff, but after 1256 when the charter forbade him to 'busy himself about anything' in Andover except the King's business, the Sheriff ceased to call this court. Instead the Men of Andover held this court twice yearly.

The first roll for 1379 records that the Alderman of the tything of Alderman de Grand reported the breaking of the assize of bread and ale by a number of innkeepers. One of them, John Craves, was fined 1s. for selling wine at too high a price namely 1s. a gallon. Two other inhabitants of the tything were fined 6d. each for selling meat which was not fresh. Inn-keepers were not licensed in those days but those before the court were fined 2s. for baking white bread or horse bread or cooking or selling meat or fish, which were described as being 'against the statute, the assize or the custom of the town'. Innkeepers could sell beer or ale to anyone but could only cook for bona fide travellers.

Some time before 1408, the Gild Merchant of Andover had begun the practice of electing two Bailiffs on the Sunday before Michaelmas. In that year the election did not proceed without incident. Three local men were summoned to appear before Henry IV and committed to prison because they 'being united together did nefariously impede the Election by litigious Expressions and most excessive shouting manifestly tending to the Disturbance and Commotion of the whole Commonalty . . .'. Henry promptly ordered a new election and directed that 'any persons . . . by confederacies, shouting, or litigious expressions, impeding' the elections should be 'without delay . . . arrested and taken and committed to the nearest prison there to remain . . .'.

While the King could commit to prison, most of the offences recorded in these early rolls were punished by fines. Occasionally other forms of punishment are used. In 1491, John Swan, 'a common malefactor' had in the night time broken down a fence and cut down ash trees belonging to his master and the neighbours. He was sentenced to the pillory, which stood in the High Street. Repaired many times, the pillory in Andover was finally abolished as a method of punishment in 1837.

The first reference to the Sergeants-at-Mace, who were officers of the Court at Andover is in 1575 when Richard Browne, one of the Sergeants, bought a horse for which he failed to pay. It was at this time too that attorneys begin to practice and one of these, Anthony Payne, complained about defamation of his character by John Knight who 'here at Andover, within the jurisdiction of the Court, falsely, maliciously and fraudulently spoke . . . "Thou doest lyve only by Pillage" to Anthony Payne in the presence of many faithfull subject of the Queen' for which he claimed damages of 39s 11d.

There were also the Church courts, of which little trace remains. One extract from the minutes of the Gild Merchant does refer to this court. When in 1456, the Twenty-Four Forwardmen ordered that gleaning should be done by hand they made the fine for breach of this order 40d payable to the Churchwardens, and the 'partyes that fyndeth ((t)hem(selves) (ag)greved thereyn take' their action in a Church Court.

There are some interesting entries in the Minute Book of the Gild Merchant; in 1574 it was agreed that 'if any of the Bailifffs or Approved Men come to Court or Lawday without his gown he shall be fined 5s.' 1577 four of the Approved Men were to accompany the Bailiff from his house to the Guildhall at every Court and sit with him all the time or be fined 3/4d.

The first mention of the office of Constable occurs in the Minutes for 1584 when the Council ordered that no-one could be elected Bailiff unless he had first been a Constable. Two Constables were elected each year and their duties were manifold as can be deduced from their accounts. They organised the watch spending 19/- on coal and 18/- on brandy and $4/10\frac{1}{2}$d on candles and 3/3 on a lanthorn in 1731. Of course they had to pay for the honour. In 1779, 10/6 was spent 'on receiving the staves' of office and only 3/- for 'Going round the town at Knight times'. In 1779 they spent 2/6d 'in Regulating at Deffrent times the Staffordshire militia' and 1/- in 'quortering the Glamorganshire militia'; but in 1780 only 7d on regulating the

'Hants Mellitia'. They also carried people out of the parish like Mary Brewer; the sum of 5/6d included some relief as well, but a further 1/- was spent at Abbotts Ann.

The Bailiffs were entitled to hold a special court for summary justice at the Markets and Fairs. Any offences at the weekly market would be brought to the next Monday court, but a dispute at Weyhill Fair could not wait, for the merchants needed to travel to the next fair. There are few records of this Pie-powder court; on 29 September 1572 the court issued three summonses for debt; on 29 September 1578 the court recorded one white wether sheep, and one sparrowhawk (on 27 September) lost, one white lamb found, a debt of 16/-, an accusation of stealing cattle and a charge of trespass. There was even less business in 1651 for none of the tythingmen reported to the Court, and all eleven of them were fined 1d each. They all came to the next four courts, but never had any complaints to make. Perhaps the Civil War had an effect on the extent of Weyhill Fair.

The legal situation was altered by the grant of the Great Charter in 1599. The freedom of the Borough or Town and Parish of Andover from the jurisdiction of the Justices of the Peace for the County of Southampton was confirmed and a weekly Court of Record was set up for Andover itself. The Views of Frankpledge Court were to be held twice yearly and the In-Hundred, Out-Hundred and Manor Courts were to continue as was the Coroner's Court. There was one exception; the Justices could not take action in cases of Murder or Felony or loss of life or member without the special command of the sovereign.

The new system meant that the pillory, the stocks and even the cage were not enough; a prison would have to be built. The accounts for the building of the prison show that it was built of timber with a tiled roof; there were iron locks and staples on the doors to both the upper and the lower prison, and the floor of the buttery which was attached to the prison was paved. Above the buttery were chambers, presumably for the gaoler. The whole cost was £116-3-4. It was started in May 1623 and finished in September 1624 when four pairs of shackles weighing 16 lb were delivered. Someone had already been incarcerated, for the glass and casement of a window had been broken by the prisoners. Contrary to popular belief of the building was near the Westbrook and not the Katherine Wheel.

One odd affair in 1642 was the dismissal of Mr Game as attorney of the Court of Record at Andover 'for certain abuses by him committed'. That was on 4 March, and on 21 March he was readmitted as an attorney on his reading an acknowledgement of his error. Quite what he said will never be known, but in those days when King Charles was at variance with his Parliament, it would be very easy to upset a Royalist with a few Parliamentary expressions.

It was during this same period of disorder that a complaint was made in the Court of the Exchequer in London about ten men of Andover who

'being persons of disordered, riotous and dissolute carriage and behaviour . . . being armed and prepared with gunnes charged with powder and shott, crossebowes, pikes, buckstalls and other unlawful weapons, netts and engines and also with greyhounds, mastives and ferretts did hunt, chase and kill . . . two bucks, . . . and the same persons during the last seven years had in like manner destroyed forty bucks, does and fawns, twenty hares, one hundred couple of coneyes, twenty pheasants, fortie partridges and other beasts . . .'. 'They deny all charges but killing 10 or 12 couple of rabbits which they understood was according to the King's wish'.

Clearly the Civil War gave some people opportunities which they might not otherwise have had.

The records of the In and Out Hundred Courts and the Court of Record continue, at times put together in the same book, at other times kept in separate books. There are three fragments of the Coroner's court which are interesting. One is the report of an inquest upon Nicholas Spackman who hanged himself with a hempen rope in Hatherden copse. Another is the tragic story of Margarett Watts and her daughter. On 30 August 1703 a panel of twelve women informed the coroner that the death of Margaret Watts and her child was 'occasioned for want of help & Assistance in her labor'. On the next day a jury of twelve men declared upon their oaths

'that the said child on Sunday the Nine and Twentieth day of August Instant about the hour of 9 in the Evening was found dead in a hole under the Staires, wrapt up in a petticoat and Shift of the said deceased Margarett Watts. They believe that the Child was born alive and afterwards murthered but know not by whome. That there was a Concealment of the fact by the Master of the House and others'

but they do not know anything more.

Another case which must have caused a great deal of excitement at the time has also been lost. Some rough notes for depositions in the case suggest that while the Corporation were electing a Bailiff in the Upper Guildhall there was considerable commotion in the space below. For instance Edward Bond was prepared to say that 'he was seat under the Town Hall in Andover aforesaid on the 10th day of Sept. last being the day of Electing a Bayliffe for the said town, and heard Mr John Gale speak to Mr Abraham Treakell the then Bayliffe In the words following, Sir, I am employed by the freemen and Inhabitants of this Town to Demand their Right of Election for Bayliffe of this Town and desires you would admit them into the Hall . . . said Abraham Treakell saying Nobody had any business there and then Ordered the Constable to keep the Doors . . . and the taking the Poll of the freemen and inhabitants . . . was Done in a Peaceable and Quiett manner without the least Disturbance or Riot whatsoever or any assault or abuse showed . . .'

James Holloway was prepared to swear that he heard 'John Joules one of the then Constables . . . Declare that if any person attempted to goe up into the Town Hall He the said John Joules would Ramm his Staffe down his the persons throat' (the last eight words were then crossed out and the words 'would knock him down' substituted). A tantalising glimpse of how town politics and criminality may go hand in hand.

Less than a hundred years later the mob did get out of hand. Economic hardship produced such distress that a wave of rioting spread across the countryside. In Andover the riots began on 19 November 1830; a threshing machine was destroyed, a prisoner taken to Andover gaol, and such a huge multitude gathered that shopkeepers closed their doors and bolted their window shutters. Then the crowd broke open the gaol and released the captive, dispersed when called upon to do so by Mr Bethel Coxe from the upper window of the 'Angel' and went on to destroy £2,000 worth of machinery at Taskers' Waterloo Foundry. Individuals or small groups burnt ricks and extorted money and food from terrified middle class families, but order was restored on 22 November when a troop of the 9th Lancers arrived. Analysis of riotous and non riotous villages suggests that those with a market, a fair, a resident lawyer and a high proportion of shoemakers—notorious radicals— were likeliest to riot; and there were 20 shoemakers in Andover.

The Municipal Reform Act of 1835 produced a number of changes in the structure of the local courts and the administration of law and order. One of the new Council's first acts, which is not recorded in the Minutes, was to petition for a separate Court of Quarter Sessions in addition to the Court of Petty Sessions. Their petition was refused by the King on the advice of his Home Secretary. The Council refused to accept this decision and prepared a second petition in which they explained how inconvenienced tradesmen and 'others in the middle Class of life' would be by having to go to distant Quarter Sessions, how reluctant they would become to prosecute, how demoralised the town would become, how much they had recently spent on a new Court room and a Gaol which was very suitable for keeping deserters being taken from Ireland to the I.O.W. and Portsmouth, and how the people of Andover were incurring heavy expenses without any benefits. They pointed out that the four magistrates recently appointed had expressed a

'disinclination to take upon themselves the arduous duties of the magistracy subject to the Interference of the Justices of the County and . . . will be reluctant in bestowing their time and attention to petty disputes and cases of assault . . . which . . . will be considerably increased by the number of Paupers and disorderly characters that will be sent to the large Workhouse now building in the Town for the Andover Parochial Union of thirty Parishes'.

The second petition was favourably considered and a Court of Quarter Sessions granted 'upon Condition that the Council will make the Borough Gaol in every respect fit and proper for the confinement of Prisoners and for the maintenance of Prison Discipline' or would arrange with the County Justices for the holding of Borough Prisoners in the County Gaol. The Council immediately set up a Committee to examine the gaol in Winchester Street, and the Town Clerk was told to find out the cost of keeping prisoners in the County Gaol. Despite their proud boasts, the Council knew that the Gaol could only hold ten prisoners, and could not accommodate those who had to be kept for the Quarter Sessions.

The Council being obliged by the Municipal Corporations Act to form a Watch Committee decided that this should consist of the whole Council. The Minutes of the Committee are lost, but the Council agreed with their recommendations to pay Watchmen a total of £13-15-6$\frac{1}{2}$ and to fix the annual salary of the Gaoler at £10. It was an unsatisfactory compromise; the Council were reluctant to spend more money than absolutely unavoidable, and yet wanted to retain a status and independence which Andover's size did not justify.

The Gaol continued to be a problem. On 17 February 1837, the Council resolved 'that it shall be at the discretion of the Magistrates to increase the allowance of the Prisoners in the Borough Gaol to the amount of sixpence per diem'. On the 29 September another committee was set up to examine the state of the Gaol, tactics which the Council employed on many other occasion. On 19 January 1838 the Council resolved 'that the Police of the Town should be made more efficient, but not by an Increase of the Borough Rate but by means of private subscriptions'. This was carried without dissent, but equally without hope of implementation. The Council came back to the question on 3 August and agreed to appoint an Official Policeman. Two Constables were appointed to serve from 1 October 1838 to 1 October 1839—they were Thomas Blake of King's Head Street, a cooper, and John Beck of High Street, a watchmaker. Clearly neither of these gentlemen could afford to be full time policemen. It is not surprising to find at that same August meeting a proposal that the two offices of Gaoler and Head Policeman should be combined at an annual salary of not more than £60.

The maintenance of prisoners at the 'County Bridewell' cost £80 for the year April 1837 to April 1838, and the conditions of the prisoners at the Borough Gaol was causing concern. In August 1838, the Council resolved that the 'Clergyman of the Established Church together with the accredited ministers of the three Dissenting Congregations in the Town' be allowed to give Religious Instruction to the Prisoners. In March 1839, the Council appointed a Committee to 'ascertain the best mode of making a sufficient airing Ground for the Prisoners'. The Committee reported in May and the work was authorised if it did not cost more than £33-1-0. In July the Council resolved to carry out the various alterations in the Borough Gaol suggested by the Inspector of Prisons. This raised the question of the Quarter Sessions again. Were there enough cases to warrant keeping the Quarter Sessions in Andover, or would it be better for the Borough, the Prisoners, and the County, if all the work were transferred to Winchester? The Council decided to retain the Quarter Sessions, to send prisoners confined for more than fourteen days to the County Gaol, and also toyed with the idea of renewing the ancient Court Leet and Court of Record in an attempt to secure speedier justice.

On 17 December 1839, the Foreman of the Grand Jury at the Quarter Sessions attended a special meeting of the Council to request the establishment of an efficient Police Force. It was in this same month that the County Police Force was established, and in April 1840 negotiations began with Captain Robbins, the Chief Constable to find out how many policeman would be stationed in Andover if the Borough agreed to merge with the County. Negotiations were short lived. In May the Council refused to join the County scheme, and in September re-appointed the two Constables with a salary of two guineas and expenses. On 5 July 1841, the Council proposed to amalgamate the Borough and County Police, suggesting the sum of £200 as the contribution from Andover and asking how many policemen would be provided. In November 1841, the County Magistrates replied that the number would be whatever was required for the protection of the 'Peace of the Town'. This was not good enough; by a majority of one the Council instead decided to appoint two efficient Constables with proper dress and accoutrements, and asked the Pavement Commission to help. The latter not only refused, but ordered the Beadle to stop doing police duty. In February 1842 a Head Constable was appointed at £1 per week, the Gaoler was given an extra £5 and his wife £5 for her services as matron at the Gaol; and there the matter rested for some time.

The In and Out Hundred Courts were still being held, though not much attention was paid to them. It would appear that the Tythingmen became very slack in their duties, and in September 1840 the Town Clerk was ordered to write to the 'Tithingmen in Arrears demanding payment of the cert money due from them at the Courts at Weyhill and Andover'. In May 1843, the Council did not consider it necessary to abolish the In and Out Hundred Courts immediately, though they admitted their inutility and unimportance'. In August they decided to discontinue them.

In August 1845 the Council agreed to appoint a Constable to reside at Charlton, thus bringing the Borough force up to 1 Head Constable, 3 Constables and 1 Gaoler. In April 1846 the Watch Committee applied through the Quarter Sessions, and the County Quarter Sessions agreed 'to maintain within the said Borough a permanent Establishment of one Sergeant and four Constables with such additional force at the time of Fairs or other occasions of unusual concourse . . .' for the sum of £325. The Council was still to pay for the maintenance of prisoners at the County Gaol, and in addition had to pay for repairs to their own gaol. This building was eventually to become the County Police Station after a protracted negotiation which began in September 1857 and was completed in February 1860. In fact before it was completed 'Third-Class Constable H. Joint was dismissed the service with one week's pay for absenting himself from his beat in Andover and being found concealed in a cupboard in a public house'.

A study of the records of the Petty Sessions Court of the period 1867–70 suggests that theft was more frequent then than now. For instance, Frederick Barnes an unemployed farm labourer was found guilty and sentenced to two months imprisonment with hard labour for theft. He was caught trying to raffle in the George at Thruxton, a number of herrings which were claimed to have been taken from a cart belonging to John Bourne, a higgler from Abbotts Ann, which was standing outside Mr Child's Brewery at Weyhill. James Wright was in prison for three months altogether for stealing three mackerel from Mrs Frith's shop. He claimed he needed them to feed his wife and family. By today's standards these are severe punishments for shoplifting.

Even youth was no obstacle to punishment. A 14 year old caught stealing turnip tops was sent to a reformatory for five years, because he had previously been caught stealing eggs. A 13 year old from Abbotts Ann was given 21 days hard labour and 6 strokes of the cane for stealing three eggs.

Cases of assault were frequent and often interesting. When Elizabeth Masters accused Emily Holt of using threatening language and throwing stones at her door, the Court was filled to capacity for the five hour hearing for 'half the female population of New Street clamoured to get into the witness box to give evidence for the defendant'.

The principal claim for the defence seems to have been that Mrs Masters grossly ill treated her children. The case was dismissed, but Emily Holt refused to pay 10/- costs and defied the Mayor when he gave her the option of paying or going to prison for 14 days. Extra police were needed to control the crowd which became very angry until some respected citizen paid the costs.

There were traffic offences. Henry Day of Hurstbourne Tarrant was fined 16/6d and 3/6d costs for riding on his cart without holding on the the reins or being at the head of it to guide the horse. Twelve shillings was the fine for riding on the shafts of a waggon. There were also fines for those who refused to pay the tolls on the turnpike.

The small detachment of Police in Andover under Sergeant Russell were sometimes sent to other parts of the county on special occasions. One of these in 1880 was at Bournemouth, where after a long day of abuse by the mob during the Guy Fawkes riots, they 'did seriously abuse their authority as police constables and by using violence where no violence was necessary' they committed the very acts it was their duty to prevent. Sergeant Russell was demoted to First-Class Constable, an action which was regretted by Alderman Moore in the Council on 1 January 1881. In reply to the minute of the Council meeting which was sent to him, the Chief Constable replied, stating 'that bearing in mind the expression of the opinion of the Council with reference to Russell's conduct while in charge of the Borough', he 'hoped to be able to shortly reinstate him in his former position'. Sergeant Russell did not return to Andover.

Trivial though such events may seem, they were important to the participants. Perhaps the people of Andover did not realise until 1914 how important an effective police force could be in preventing damage. In June 1914 a lot of Upper High Street glass, mainly shop windows was broken in a riot which began in New Street over an unpopular affiliation order decision. Excitement and the hysteria of being part of a mob resulted in an outbreak of violence in the High Street on Friday evening which was not calmed down till 3 a.m. on Saturday when police reinforcements arrived from Winchester. Another outbreak occurred on Saturday evening after the public houses emptied, but this only lasted until 1 a.m. when mounted police had managed to cordon off the High Street. On Sunday the rioters moved down to Charlton Road, but scattered when police approached and though they thronged the High Street looking for more excitement, there was none. The seriousness of the riot was due to the fact that only one sergeant and two constables were available on Friday evening. 'If twenty men had joined in assisting the police the first outbreak would have been speedily quelled and the town saved a 3d rate . . . The cost of the extra police alone may be a little lesson to those who pay the rates not to encourage disorder'. The 'Andover Advertiser' remarked on the bad name given to the town by exaggerated reports of the proceedings and also on the adverse effect to Andover's trade.

The most notorious crime in the area took place on the road at Thruxton Down in 1920 when a taxi driver was hired by Percy Topliss to drive him from Salisbury to Andover Junction station. The taxi driver was shot, robbed and his body concealed in the hedge, but his murderer was finally cornered and shot in a gun battle with the police at Penrith, Cumbria. The murder spot on the A303 is often referred to as Topliss Hill.

For many years Petty Sessions and Quarter Sessions were held in the Court Room or Council Chamber in the Guildhall, which was not always as pleasant as it might have been. After complaints, the Council agreed on 7 December 1878 to 'rearrange the present fittings of the Sessions Court to render the same more commodious for magisterial and other public purposes.'

As the business of the Courts grew with increased legislation and population, both natural events, the disadvantages of the accommodation became more pronounced. The Old Police Station in Winchester Street, which had been the Borough Gaol, was still in use until 30 September 1959 when a new Police Station of more modern and spacious style was opened in a position slightly nearer the Town Centre. But the Courtroom in the Guildhall was still very crowded and undignified with witnesses, defendants, police, solicitors, ushers and others tripping over themselves on the staircase. Even the termination of the Borough Quarter Sessions and the amalgamation of the bench of Justices for Town and County made no difference.

The new Court House built in 1974 and officially opened in 1976 is immeasurably more spacious and dignified. Two large formal Court rooms panelled in wood with orange or green upholstery, enable most cases to be heard in comfort and care. Two smaller and less formal courtrooms are available, one used for juveniles, and there is space for solicitors, the press and the general public. One whole section of the building is used by the Probation and After-Care Services. Andover can be proud of this building in which Justice can 'lift aloft her scales'.

Andover Police Station 1860 to 1959.

Chapter Eight
COMMON ACRE

'. . . his pride is in Picquette,
New-market-fame, and judgement at a Bett.'

The origin of 'Common Acre' is still unknown; the reason why the narrow strip of land lying between the avenue of limes became the recreation ground for the people of Andover more than 500 years ago cannot be determined positively. It may have been a royal grant to the 'Men of Andover', for the 'Town Barn' stood at its lower end; it may be that it was a neglected headland on the limit of the East Field nearest to the Church. It never belonged to Katherine Hanson, despite the statement of the Benefactions Tablet.

The daily life of the average inhabitant of Andover during the Middle Ages would be one of hard labour, but broken by Sundays and frequent Saints Days and, of course, the three Town Fairs. On Sundays attendance at Church was obligatory, and even sometimes after the Reformation, when a greater degree of freedom prevailed, the records of the courts are littered with accusations of non-attendance. Sometimes it was even worse: 'we present John Hatchet for suffering tippling in his house in the time of divine service and therfor forfetts the sume of ten shillings and John Hullett for tippling their therefor forfetts 3s 4d' reads the court record for 1 August 1642.

After the customary attendance at Divine Service on Sunday, came the equally obligatory, but less well documented practice of archery, which was ordained in 1542 by Henry VIII because the number of skilful archers had declined since the fourteenth century when the long bow had first proved its usefulness. National Service, in the form of practice at the butts was to come second to religious observance, and for the men of Andover the most convenient practice ground was the strip nearest the church. It may have happened that since the practice of archery had been pursued there, for one season while the East Field was fallow, Common Acre became permanent fallow or pasture, while the remainder of the field continued to produce crops.

In the earliest lease of Common Acre for pasture, Robert Maynsak and Thomas Hode agreed in 1470 to allow 'everyone of good governance and conversation to play at spears and arrows and other games' and to pass through the land during the day without interruption. Leases of later times had similar clauses. In 1513 the lease to Thomas Alred stipulated that the tenant was to set up the butts; 'as has been anciently accustomed' was added to this provision when the lease was granted to Edward Marten in 1540. The lease in 1560 is even more detailed: William Good is to 'kepe make and maynteyne one pair of butts there mete for men to shoote at' and 'to suffer all manner of persons to come and goe in to and from the said premises to shote and have theire pastyme there as it hath been accustomed'.

Frequent complaints were registered in later years about the decay of the butts; this is hardly surprising in view of the changeover to power assisted missiles which followed the introduction of gunpowder. From 1600 onwards, muskets, corslets and gunpowder appear more frequently in the accounts of the Town Chamberlain. The responsibility of the town to provide one armed soldier was often discharged on different occasions by the same man. On one occasion in 1626, the training session for Hampshire was held on Common Acre, and the accounts show that Thomas Godden received 4d for his one day's service.

The decline of archery altered the recreational use of Common Acre. A lease in 1660 to Humphrey Painter required him to restrict his pasturing to sheep and lambs only, and to keep them off the bowling green which was the upper end of Common Acre, railed off from 31 March to 30 September. Another clause in the same lease absolved the tenant from the repair of fences damaged by soldiery. By 1786, the lease reserved 'liberty for the inhabitants and others to walk and recreate themselves as usual', from which it would seem that the use of Common Acre for sports and organised games had been abandoned. Common Acre was still used for special occasions, as for example in 1799 and again in 1802 when the ringleaders of the riots by some soldiers quartered in Andover were flogged in public after a Court Martial.

Where also then did the 'men of Andover' take their pleasures? It seems likely that there had always been a number of illegal alehouses. Selling food and drink to bona fide travellers was not an offence and inns such as the Angel, Bell, Star and Katherine Wheel catered for genuine travellers. Bakers were permitted to sell cooked food to residents of the town but there were many places in Andover where food and drink were sold illegally because the consumers were residents. In the sixteenth century a system of licensing these alehouses was introduced, and provided the licensee conducted an orderly house there was no trouble. Perhaps one can sympathise with Dorothy Pearce a widow for not choosing the right customers. She was in trouble on 9 February 1642 for 'keeping ill Orders in her howse att unseasonable tymes in the night & giving entertaynment to some which did abuse the watch'.

Of course it was necessary to obey the law; on 1 August 1642 at the View of Frankpledge—

'We present Robert Drewe, Edward Summersett, John Hatchett, John Prince, George Smith, Edward Chode, Judeth Cooke, John Browne, Richard Junkins, Robert Smith, William S(c)ullard, John Elton, John Warner, Robert Dynes, Alice Pitman, Joane Cooke, Michael Bulles ('Bold'), Mris. Mary Pope, John Rathband, John Channoll, Lewis Fiesed, Gyles Tompkins, William Duneford, William Juliance, Roger Bird, John Chariett, John Stockes, for not selling A full Alle quart of the best beere for A penny contrary to the Statute in that cause made and provided therfor forfeit 20s. apeece'.

Much of the High Street and Bridge Street must have consisted of licensed alehouses in the seventeenth century; Gyles Tompkins was later licensed to sell wine from the 'Bell', as was Mrs Pope at the 'Angel'.

Some of the eighteenth century alehouses were noted for special features. Skittles, for instance, was played at the 'Jolly Farmer' in Bridge Street, and at the 'Marquis of Granby' which fronted Common Acre. The best known was 'Bowling Green House', renamed 'Antelope' and later still 'Folly Inn'. The bowling green is marked on the Tithe Map of 1848, on an island in the Charlton road.

Another licensed house had a different but undeserved reputation. At some distance from the centre of the town on the London Road stands the 'Queen Charlotte'. In the sloping field at the rear of the Inn, prize fights are supposed to have been held. In fact the venue was normally two miles away at Finkley Down. The most notorious was in 1832 when Owen Smith fought Anthony Noon at Hurstbourne Tarrant Common. Noon was battered so mercilessly that he died later that evening at the 'Katherine Wheel'. Smith was tried for manslaughter at Winchester Assizes and was jailed for six months. On the east side of the 'Queen Charlotte' is a turfed area which was a skittle alley, and cock fighting was staged in the yard a century or so ago. Beyond the 'Queen Charlotte' was the racecourse, on the edge of Harewood Forest. This is marked on Isaac Taylor's map of 1759, but no race cards or details of the races have been preserved through it is probable that they were run at times of the Fairs. Nor are there any details of the Andover Cricket Week which became a custom about 1790. Perhaps this feature was an imitation of earlier matches played on Perham Down, and it would have been more likely to have involved the leisured classes, that is the country gentry and their retainers rather than the working men or shopkeepers of Andover.

On the other hand, the shopkeepers and working men played the leading roles in the Andover Volunteers, the Andover Yeomanry Cavalry, and the Loyal Andover Volunteers. The enthusiasm which supported these part-time militia units sprang from disgust at the initial excesses of the French Revolution, and there was probably considerable disappointment that they were only needed in the 1798 emergency as a stand-by force. Local rivalry accounted for the number of different units.

For a short period there was a theatre in Andover, a specially constructed building with folding doors, above which appeared the words 'Theatre Royal' in large letters while 'From the' and 'Windsor' on either side were almost invisible. As might be expected the performances were of the 'rehearsal in the provinces' type; on one occasion, the actors would not perform so long as a copy of the play was being consulted by a member of the audience. The theatre opened in January 1803 on the site of the old stables of Priory Lodge,—now an access road—and was still open in 1805. No doubt it closed shortly afterwards for there was no regular company but only infrequent visitations at the whim of the manager.

If the people of Andover were deprived of theatrical experiences, there was a library of sorts. Quite when it started is unknown; possibly it was a by-product of the Reform Movement of the early nineteenth century. A Minute of the Town Council for 3 May 1844 allowed the Trustees of the Andover Library to place a book case in the Council Room. No further mention is made of this book case, but it was probably taken over by the Mechanics Institute which appears in Andover in the 1860s. Proudly, perhaps, the Institute printed a catalogue of its reading material compiled by the oddly named librarian, Mr Drinkwater Butt. Nearly half the catalogue is devoted to novels and tales.

When the Mechanics Institute, which had been established in the 'Katherine Wheel', ran into financial trouble, the trustees offered the land, building and books to the Council for £500 with which to pay off their own shareholders. The project aroused bitter controversy because money was needed. Alterations to the building would cost a further £773 and no one wanted to raise the rates. The original purchase was financed by a gift of £500 from Alfred Butterworth, a Lancastrian businessman living at Hatherden House, and the alterations by a gift of £500 from Hampshire County Council, £200 from a subscription list and £73 from the proceeds of a bazaar. The Freedom of the Borough was conferred on Alfred Butterworth at the opening of the Free Library on 11 July 1899, when it was revealed that he had also given the 'best 100 books'—presumably a standard collection—which the Mayor hoped the 'lads would read and benefit from'. For five years the Library was Free, but in 1903 the managers had to ask for help from the rates, which solved the anomalous position. The library stayed beside the river until 1972.

The Mechanics Institute was not the only literary institution; there was a Working Men's Club in the 1860s which advertised subscriptions to weekly and monthly magazines, as well as facilities for fencing and bagatelle. It was probably from this source that the news was spread of the codification of the laws of Association Football in 1863. On 18 December, the 'Advertiser' announced its pleasure at finding 'the Volunteers of Andover are turning their attention to this manly game'. The essential item of equipment was a football and a fund to purchase one to be used by the 'civilians' of Andover was announced the following January. After considerable practice, a match—the first recorded match—was held on 2 December 1864 between the Acre Club (red) and the Andover Football Club (blue). As it was played at the cricket ground, at that time at Shepherd's Springs, there was a natural disagreement before the game began over the position of the goals. Andover won 2–1.

All games before 1869 were played to local rules, and an inter-town match with Romsey played in 1868 at the Walled Meadow ground caused considerable controversy and delay in the progress of the game. The Romsey team's method of 'shouldering' was considered by Andover to be contrary to the laws of the game, and enthusiasm lapsed until 1883.

There was a most important change in leisure time activities in 1870 with the introduction of Early Closing. Until then, there had been no regular opportunity for daylight sports except on Sundays in defiance of Victorian morality. For the shopworkers at least, there was from 1870 at least one early evening when they were not forced to stay in the shop. There was some delay in realising the full benefits of Early Closing, which was perfectly natural.

James Witton, a Lancastrian by birth, and Headmaster of the Free Grammar School from 1880, led the resurgence of footballing enthusiasm. On Monday 25 September 1883 a public meeting at the Guildhall agreed to form the Andover Football Club. A practice match was held in Mr Stride's meadow in Weyhill Road between an XI captained by Mr Tanner, and 'the next XV' captained by Rev J. C. Witton. The first friendly game with Basingstoke Engineers on 27 October was reported in the 'Advertiser': 'The visitors displayed a marked inclination for obstreperousness and what was more to be regretted they more than once disputed the Andover umpire's (Rev J. C. Witton) decision in language that was anything but gentlemanly . . . we cannot too strongly condemn some of the language used.'

From 1887 to 1962 the Andover Football Club played in the Hampshire League and were the only club in the county with an unbroken record. During this time they won every trophy, some more than once. In their final year in the league the two teams won both First and Second Division championships. The opposition in the Western and Southern Leagues has been much tougher.

To celebrate Queen Victoria's Golden Jubilee in 1887, the Corporation bought from Winchester College the piece of land which lay alongside Common Acre. The whole area was turned into a Recreation Ground and devoted to open air activity, but because of the peculiar origin of Common Acre, the children's swings, and roundabouts, could not be placed thereon nor could the bandstand. Bonfires are allowed on Common Acre, though perhaps not as big as the large bonfire built to celebrate the Golden Jubilee. A new bandstand with a central iron column, later transformed into an aviary, was given by Alderman E. C. Lovell in 1930, the year in which he was Mayor.

THE

ANNUAL PINK FEAST,

WILL BE HELD AT THE

WHITE HART INN, ANDOVER,

On ~~FRIDAY~~ *Tuesday* JULY 3rd, 1832,

WHEN THE FOLLOWING PRIZES WILL BE GIVEN.

—»»◉●◐●«—

The Person who shows NINE of the best whole blown Flowers of different sorts, will be entitled to a piece of Plate, value..................... }	3	10	0
The SECOND BEST, ...	2	10	0
The THIRD BEST,...........................	1	10	0
The FOURTH BEST,.	1	0	0

ALSO, A MAIDEN PRIZE.

To the Person who shows SIX of the best whole blown Flowers of different sorts, value........ }	1	0	0

—»»◉●◐●«—

All Persons will be sworn that the Flowers are their own Property,
and have been in their Possession three Months last past.

STEWARDS

MR. T. HEATH AND MR. WAKEFORD.

Mr. F. BAILEY, TREASURER.

The Prizes to be determined by three Umpires, chosen by the majority of the Company.

No Person to be permitted to show, who has not subscribed 5s. three Months previous to showing, unless he subscribes 10s. at the time of showing.

☞ *No Person to show unless he dines or pays for his Dinner.*

N. B. DINNER ON TABLE AT TWO O'CLOCK.

King, Printer, Andover.

For many years a section of the river near Anton Mill had been used as a swimming place. Under the Baths and Washhouses Act, this became the responsibility of the Town Council in 1876. For a few years they maintained it, but as it became expensive to repair, so did their reluctance to raise the rates for such a purpose. After 1881, it was not used. In 1885 an indoor swimming pool was opened in Beale's Building Yard in Adelaide Road. The building had a dual purpose; in winter it was boarded over and used for balls and theatrical performances. The enterprising owner, Mr Beale, offered to supply cheaper swimming facilities on Saturday nights between June and September if the Council would subsidise it at the rate of £1 per week, which they did. As the water was changed on Sundays, it will be appreciated that Saturday night was not popular with the more fastidious client. The building and yard were gutted by fire in March 1894, rebuilt in similar fashion, and demolished in 1975.

In the later years of the century several other sporting clubs were formed. A Hockey Club in 1895 and several cricket clubs to be followed by a Golf Club in 1907, a Bowling Club in 1919, and so on. None of them has produced any Olympic or World Champions, though a number of athletes have competed in Internationals. The open air swimming pool which was opened in 1936 in a very convenient position at the upper end of London Street was not of Olympic dimensions, and has now been replaced by a large covered swimming pool which is part of the Cricklade sports complex.

Rural populations have always cultivated their own plots, but the urban growth of Andover in the nineteenth century made this impossible for some dwellers in the more crowded streets. Allotments of land have been provided wherever convenient, and in this more prosaic way carries on the tradition of the early nineteenth century when there was an Annual Pink Feast.

Even before Town Development, new playing fields had been provided by the Council, but the advent of an increasing population made more space for recreation essential. The building of a sports hall next to the new swimming pool in the Cricklade complex means that Andover can now boast of more than adequate sports facilities. There may be no dirt track or greyhound stadium, but few towns of Andover's size have such facilities. The completion of a Leisure Centre planned for Charlton will provide such varied facilities for recreation that would astound our forefathers, limited to shooting, archery, walking, bowling or conversing on Common Acre.

Programme for the Annual Pink Feast.

Chapter Nine
THE OLD GRAMMAR SCHOOL

"Tis Education forms the common mind
Just as the Twig is bent, the Tree's inclin'd.'

Few travellers using the New Street ring-road realise that the undignified clutter of red brick and tile and black iron railings between them and the church is the unexciting back of what was for many young people the most important building in Andover. Set into its front, facing Church Close, is a foundation stone recording the erection of the new classrooms in 1888. These filled the playground space adjoining the old Schoolhouse, which before it became a school in 1848, had been a private house for just over a century.

An earlier Schoolhouse had been built in 1624 at the outer corner of the churchyard, whence the lucky scholars could, if circumstances permitted, witness some of the exciting events which happened in Andover through the windows overlooking the main London Road. Whether the school is much earlier is unlikely—there is no certain evidence for any educational institution earlier than 1569.

While some of the sixteenth century tradesmen of Andover were unable to sign their names, there were many who could, and some who could read, write and cypher. Only thirty one Andover boys are listed on the scholars roll of Winchester College for the period 1393–1570. Any young Andover boy wishing to enter the church— and several are recorded in the Registers of the Bishops of Winchester—would probably receive his earliest instruction in reading and singing from the priest of the Chantry or from the monks of the Priory. The existence in 1446 of a Luke Scholemaystre with a holding in Wode Street and an acre near the chalkpits is no proof of a school in Andover.

Like many other towns in the sixteenth century, Andover felt the need for a real school of its own. Unlike so many similar schools, the date of foundation of the Free Grammar School of Andover is surrounded by controversy. It is certain that John Hanson, in his will made in 1571 just before he died, left the residue of his property 'for the use of a free school', which further on he explained as the 'erection of a schoolhouse' and the proviso that the schoolmaster should be a graduate of Oxford or Cambridge, at a salary of not less than £16 p.a. The wording in his will suggests that he had already given £200 to Bishop Horne for this purpose, and the Bishop passed the money to William Blake as a loan at 8%, but exact dates are not known for these transactions.

Who founded the school is therefore uncertain. John Hanson was certainly one of the earliest benefactors. The badge used by the Free Grammar School was a rebus, or pictorial pun on his name. Other early benefactors were Richard Kemis who added another £5 to the schoolmaster's salary, Richard Blake who in 1624 conveyed a house and garden 'newly erected and built in London Lane, next to the Churchyard on the north of the street' to be used as a school; and Rev Hugh Marshall, one of the first schoolmasters, who left his library of books to the school.

For many years, the Free School seems to have been the only academic institution in Andover, and its condition varied with the character of its schoolmaster. A particularly detailed idea of the character of the school under the control of Rev Thomas Griffiths (1776–1798) can be gained from the memoirs of Henry 'Orator' Hunt.

Griffith's sadistic methods were so irrational that Hunt finally ran away to his father at Enford near Upavon; he would have been sent back to Andover, if his father had not received a letter from Mr Griffith 'couched in the most coarse and unfeeling language. . . . Within two years of this time, Griffiths' school dwindled down to nothing, and soon afterwards, execrated by every boy that had ever been under his care, he returned to Wales.' Hunt's opinion was that the Grammar School was 'a stain upon and a disgrace to the character of English education; in Scotland . . . the master would have been indicted.' Griffith's end is unknown, unlike Mr Chapman, organist and master of the Central School at Andover who during the great frost of January and February of 1814 was found frozen to death near Wallop.

There were numerous small boarding establishments in Andover in the mid nineteenth century. Seven young ladies stayed at Mrs Pool's in Bridge Street, while ten young ladies attended Hillside House Academy in the Weyhill Road. Eleven boys attended a boarding school in the High Street, and eight more in Sopers Lane. The biggest school was Mrs Maude's where there were nineteen

89

young ladies, one from as far away as Lincolnshire. The Free Grammar School had six boarders and a number of day boys.

While the Free Grammar School was housed in the angle of Newbury Street and New Street it was incapable of growth. It might have fallen into complete decay as many other similar schools did in the early nineteenth century, were it not for the benefaction of Miss Martha Gale. A lady of small stature and an exceedingly cheerful presence, she was the niece of Dr W. S. Goddard, for whom she kept house after her aunt's death. A substantial heiress after her uncle's death, she arranged to purchase nearly an acre of land further along New Street where a substantial house of 1740 already stood, and to exchange this for the old school master's house and school. The Charity Trustees received the new premises on 5 October 1848, and agreed to have a new schoolroom added at Miss Gale's expense. Her purpose in making this exchange was to enable her to pull down the old schoolmaster's house and schoolroom which stood between her house—the Priory,—and the new church paid for by her uncle.

Not content with this benevolence, Miss Gale also endowed in 1852 a School of Industry for Andover girls on a site next to the new church. Here behind knapped flint and stone walls, up to twelve girls aged between 12 and 15 were boarded, clothed and instructed in basic subjects, English, Religious Instruction and Domestic Economy, at her own expense. Her motives were not altruistic, for her school supplied domestic servants who already knew the requirements of their job. The numbers of girls dwindled in the twentieth century, and finally the School of Industry was closed and the endowment transferred to 'Miss Gale's Educational Foundation' which was intended to help any scholar of an Andover school under 25, but preferably a girl.

Miss Gale's third benefaction was an infants school also in 1852 in Church Hill where in 1870, 96 children of both sexes were taught by a schoolmistress. An annual sum of £20 was available for the school, and in later years it became an annex for the Church of England School in East Street; it closed in 1935.

In addition to the private schools, there was also a National School which was denominational, and a British School which was not. It would be unfair to describe Andover as being backward in providing education for the children of the area. If the information supplied to the census takers in 1851 was accurate then at least two thirds of the children aged between 4 and 14 were at school. Not that every parent was satisfied. Mrs Scammel was certainly not pleased with the schoolmaster of the National School when her son John was kept back for 15 minutes for having been caught out in a lie. She 'unreasonably insisted that he was totally incapable of falsehood, totally disbelieving my own correct statement' as the Headmaster noted in his log book for 19 May 1864. She objected again in November when he was kept in to learn his task, and came in on the next school day and took him away.

The National School had been started in 1818, but the present buildings in East Street were designed in 1859 by William White of Wimpole Street. Two houses for the master and mistress were sandwiched between the boys' school on the north and the girls' and infants' departments on the south. The British Schools had been started in 1834 in Rack Close, now Eastfield Road, and moved after a

West elevation of the Andover British School, 1859.

disastrous fire to a site in New Street where a smaller version of the National School design was produced by William Gue. It differed in having a bell tower as well as a louvred spire, and there was more ornate brickwork in the walling, and a set of privies at the back of the playing yard. The yard was divided by a wall though there was no separation internally between the girls' schoolroom and the boys' schoolroom. Details of the desks were similar in both schools.

The school year for the National School began on 8 September 1862, though attendance did not reach average until the end of the month, and dropped again in November when there was a lot of sickness. The Christmas Holidays were from 19 December to 4 January, and the master noted a lower attendance in the spring on wet days. There was a holiday in March when the Prince of Wales married, and the Easter Holiday, one week, was followed by holidays for May 13—Mayday, May 14—Ascension Day, June 18—half holiday for Waterloo, and 29 June for Coronation. Attendance was thin on 1 June for 'local causes viz. Charlton Club', and of course during the haying time. School broke up on 31 July for the harvest. During the year, Rev H. R. Richards visited the school every Friday to examine a class in some subject, and there was also a monthly visitor, one of the managers. In 1866 the Inspector reported 'The boys are well behaved but rather dull. They do not show much intelligence or thoughtfulness in their answers'. Perhaps he came on a bad day, for in 1867 he wrote 'The Boys are in good order & I am glad to find a great improvement in their intelligence since last year'.

The situation in Andover was such that no School Board was needed in 1870. The Town Clerk kept a copy of his answers to the returns required by the Educational Statistics Branch of the Home Office. On Form 72 he estimated the population of Andover as 5,550 and its rateable value as £21,841-13-11; though as owners of cottages worth less than £8 did not pay rates, there were only 843 ratepayers. The returns from the thirteen primary schools show that 483 boys and 492 girls were on the rolls of the various schools. Of these, 29 were under 3 years old, 491 between 3 and 7 years old, 421 between 8 and 13 and 34 who were 14 and over. This figure does not include the scholars of the Free Grammar School. There were also 194 attenders at Night Schools, 19 girls and the rest boys, 134 being between 14 and 21, and 10 over 21.

Every school taught reading and writing, and most taught arithmetic and scripture. Dictation, History, Grammar, Geography and Needlework were taught at the National School, the British School, Hatherden School (no Grammar) and Smannell (no Grammar or History) and the Union Workhouse School. In addition the British School had 47 pupils taking Music, 116 taking Drawing, 62 for Composition, and 36 for Domestic Economy. As might be expected, the curriculum at the Union Workhouse was more pragmatic; 13 took Laundry and Housework, 6 were taught Mapping, 2 Shoemaking, and 3 Tailoring. The National Girls School Log book suggests that Drawing was also taught, but it rather depended upon the punctual arrival of the Drawing Master. Some of the ladies of the Management Committee helped to dispose of the needlework which formed a considerable part of the school's output. On occasions they even took lessons. Singing was an important feature of school—sometimes secular songs, but frequently hymn practice which no doubt raised the standard of the Sunday School. When the Master of the British School who had been there for four years moved on, the 'Advertiser' printed a fulsome piece on 31 May 1872.

'Mr Thorne, being about to leave Andover, having been appointed master of the Training School for Teachers at Madagascar, was presented at the school on Thursday with a handsome set of nine volumes of Carlyle's works voluntarily subscribed for by the boys and girls mistress and other friends as a testimony of their esteem and respect.'

The provisions of the 1876 Education Act forced the Borough Council to take action. To every house in the Borough including Wildhern and Enham, the Mayor distributed a pamphlet explaining the new act, and on 6 January 1877 the School Attendance Committee held its first meeting. The setting up of the machinery took some time. The School Attendance Officer reported that there were 550 children of compulsory school age in Andover, and a further 200 in Charlton, Hatherden and Smannell. The first summons for neglecting to send a child to school was ordered but not issued in September. It was a successful threat despite an attempt to show that the child in question was of 'impaired intellect'.

One of the early problems was the payment of fees—the weekly penny—which the poorer parents were unable to afford. The Poor Law Guardians were supposed to support the poorer children with finance, but had to be stirred into action. Another problem was the refusal of some schools to admit children because of the untidy or dirty state of their clothing. Sometimes the parent was working away from home and the warning could not be given. The first fine for refusal to obey an attendance order was 2/6d paid by Henry Shears in December 1878. He was fined again in May and July 1879 and June 1880.

In May 1881, the Police Committee in Winchester tried to stop the Andover Police from being involved in the enforcement of School Attendance Orders, but as the Andover Police were still nominally controlled by the Borough Watch Committee, Attendance Orders and sometimes distress warrants continued to be enforced by the Andover Constabulary.

The problems of the School Attendance Officer were only part of the story. The schools had their own problems. The British School had difficulty with staff. Miss Willis of Clatford, appointed in October 1896 resigned in April 1897 on the grounds of ill health. She was followed by Miss Blacklock of Harrington, Cumberland, who resigned in 1898, and Miss Mary Redpath of Dublin, who lasted two months, November 1899—January 1900. When Miss Saunders from Evercreech National School was appointed on 17 February 1900 she demanded £26 worth of materials, Reading Books, Arithmetics, Stationery and Materials for Needlework. Although they were supplied she did not stay and was succeeded by Miss Wonnersely of Shipley.

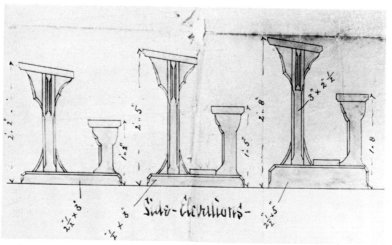

Architect's plan for the National School desks, 1859.

Part of the trouble may have been jealousy of the Boys' side. Here the Headmaster was Mr Gale, whose salary was increased by £10 p.a. in 1898, to a total of £170. This compares very favourably with the 5/- weekly paid to the monitress. Mr Gale seems to have had considerable domestic trouble; he was away from school for two terms and was then allowed to begin at 10 a.m. when school began at 9 a.m. When his debts increased beyond his capacity to pay, and his salary had been drawn in advance for some time, the Trustees asked him to leave because they refused to pay bills for his personal needs which he had run up with the Educational Supply Association.

The Infants department also suffered: when the whole school was closed by an order from the Urban Sanitary Authority in January 1898 because of an epidemic of influenza and measles, the Infants remained closed when the Boys and Girls reopened. Unlike the National Schools which were strongly Church of England the British Schools had no denominational bias and no endowment or supporting organisation. It was financed until 1902 by the weekly fees, the Government grant and a share of a joint collection of subscriptions from the wealthier sections of Andover.

The transformation of the Mechanics Institute into the Public Libary left a gap in Adult Education. In 1891, the County Council, using its powers under the Technical Instruction Act, hired the lower part of the Town Hall one night a week for a woodwork class. The following year, cookery classes were held at 2/- per night. The same Act stimulated activity at the Free Grammar School where the new classroom block had been completed. The Governors resolved in November 1892 to superintend and manage a Science School, and asked the Board of Education to recognise the Headmaster as eligible for payments for successes obtained by his Science pupils.

The Balfour Education Act of 1902 changed the whole pattern of education in Andover. The County Council refused the Borough Council's application for delegated powers, and took over control of all elementary schools, financing them from the county rates. The Free Grammar School, as an Endowed school was beyond the County's control, but representatives from the County Council, joined the Charity Trustees on the Governing Body. Some free places at the Grammar School were paid for by the County, and offered to local children whose ability merited their selection. The rest continued at their local school; the National School became the East Street (C of E Endowed) School; the old British School became New Street School.

In 1925 the Grammar School moved out of its buildings in New Street and amalgamated with Miss Reynold's private school known as the High School, Weyhill Road. The latter building was purchased by the County Council and used as a boarding department for twelve girls. There were also twenty-eight girls from the Pupil Teachers' Centre which was housed in the Art School above the Library in Bridge Street, and so seventy-nine girls joined 105 boys in a new co-educational Grammar School in new buildings on a new site in Weyhill Road.

The old Headmaster's House was sold to A. C. Bennett, but the classrooms were later used for New Street School. Soon afterwards a Senior School for boys was built on what had been the old playing fields of the Grammar School—their cricket pavilion still stands in a forgotten corner—in London Road, and shortly afterwards a Girls' Senior School was opened on the other side of London Road. Then the Butler Act of 1944 created three secondary schools, one Grammar and two Modern.

During World War II and until the late 1950s, the Andover Community Association played a considerable part directly and indirectly in the cultural life of the town. Starting originally as a 'Forum' for fortnightly debates, it extended its activities to encompass a Drama Group, Music Group, Playreading and Literary Circles, History Group, Dancing and Language Classes. Operating from hired premises—it never achieved a home of its own—it offered people of varied interests a chance to meet for a common purpose. Although the Association withered, the component parts grew in number and variety.

New housing developments increased the need for schools. To cater for children living near the Weyhill Road, Portway Junior and Infant Schools were opened. Two more schools, Vigo Road Junior and Infants were built to take children from the eastern part of the town. Wolversdene School was transferred to a site further south in 1968 and divided between Anton Junior and Infant Schools. At the same time a new school was built on the Salisbury Road, and the children from New Street School became the first members of Balksbury Junior and Infant Schools. A special School, Norman Gate School, occupied the old Grammar School buildings for a few years until a purpose built unit was ready on the Vigo Road site. Another Special School, Icknield School, was built on the Newbury Road.

A new Secondary Co-educational School opened in 1967 on a large site alongside the Harroway, whence its name. Two more Primary Schools, Shepherds' Spring Junior and Infants opened on the northern side of the town. These were followed by Knights Enham Junior and Infant Schools and Roman Way School, both north of the town and St John the Baptist (R.C.) School to the west. Reorganisation of secondary education was carried through in 1974. The two ex-senior schools became one large comprehensive, matching Harroway which had reached full size. Andover Grammar School became John Hanson comprehensive and all three schools were limited to the 11–16 age range. A new concept, a Sixth Form College was specially built on a site at Cricklade where for many years the organisation of Adult Education had been carried on.

Meanwhile, the old Grammar School still stands, a large and complex building convenient for the Town Centre, though remote from the residential areas, for which a new use has been found. Part of it is used as a Teachers' Centre where lectures and exhibitions of new materials can be held so that the children of Andover will continue to receive that up to date teaching which lay behind John Hanson's original gift of £200.

Chapter Ten
THE ALMSHOUSES

'He feeds yon Almshouses, neat, but void of state,
Where Age and Want sit smiling at the gate:
Him portion'd maids, apprentic'd orphans blest,
The young who labour, and the old who rest.'

A pair of red brick and knapped flint cottages with their backs to the roundabout and their faces to a car park are the visible evidence of the charitable impulses of four centuries ago. When they were built in Jacobean times, between 1622 and 1647, they faced the Town Barn at the bottom of Common Acre, and backed on to the garden of the later 'Rats Castle'. Rebuilt in 1869 when the thatched roof was replaced by tiles, there were four houses with a porch for the door of the central pair, though frequently they housed nine or more persons; modern conditions have made them suitable for only two pensioner families.

Another row of almshouses 'The Blew Almshouses' used to be occupied by six 'poor ancient men' at the foot of Church Hill. Built in brick and flint by John Pollen in 1686 they had been extensively repaired in the nineteenth century and were finally sold by public auction in 1975.

These were the buildings which expressed the charitable intentions of some Andover folk; for some it was a Christian duty to help the poor, for some it was a question of local pride, or personal prestige, and for some it was a way of giving thanks for their commercial success. For whatever motive or motives inspired their gifts, through the natural inexperience of well meaning but non-meticulous accountants, the value of the original gifts became impaired. When the Parliamentary Commissioners for inquiring concerning Charities came to look into the affairs of Andover, they commented upon this lamentable deficiency. Their report, published in 1825 was as comprehensive a document as they could make. Some of the details which they could not locate have since been discovered among the archives. In addition, the Charity Commissioners were almost certainly misled as have been successive generations of townsfolk, by the 'Benefactions Tablet'.

During the Middle Ages, both St Mary's Church and the Chantry benefited from the duty and obligation of the Christian faithful to give alms. The Reformation altered the destination of many of these gifts, for puritanism clashed with the ornate decoration of church interiors. In the post Reformation period gifts for educational purposes became a fashionable alternative to gifts for the benefit of the poor. John Hanson's gift was similar in intention to those of his contemporaries who endowed schools, like Dauntsey at Devizes and Blundell at Tiverton.

In the earliest surviving accounts of the Town Chamberlains, namely for 1513–1535, there is no indication of any distribution of alms for the poor, but in the 1598–1605 accounts payments for the town's business, for example a 'sugar loaf for my Lord Sandys', a fee for trimming the mace and 'sisinge the measures', nails, boards and work, are mixed with payments for bread often baked by 'Goodwyfe Ashleye' and a note to pay fourpence weekly to fifteen poor people from 15 March 1600. The two Chamberlains were supposed to keep an eye on each other's records, but this does not seem to have worked very well. A turning point was reached in 1618 when it was decided that each of the two Chamberlains should be responsible for one part of the payments; one for the Town, the other for 'Charitable Uses'. Although the two accounts were supposed to be separate, Andrew Twitchin's Accounts for 1618–22 as Town Chamberlain still record payments to Widow Ashly for bread, £5 to the Bailiff for the 'poore on Ash Wednesday' and £6 to the Schoolmaster, suggesting that the separation was incomplete. Probably setting up a separate organisation was more involved than at first imagined. For example, John Hanson's £200 which Bishop Horne lent to William Blake about 1570 had still not been repaid by 4 June 1610 when the Corporation issued a strong warning to William Blake about it.

To add to this non repayment, the Corporation now found that it had to find some way of using £400 left to it by Richard Kemis by will dated 25 September 1611, eleven days before his death. Richard Venables had left £100 in his will proved in 1598 to provide weekly doles of bread to the poor, and the trustees had allowed the Corporation to use the principal and pay the interest from the Corporation's revenue, which was not a satisfactory alternative to a loan at interest to a third party. The number of third parties who could usefully use even a part of the Kemis £400 was limited, and the decision was taken to purchase property for renting.

In 1613 the Corporation purchased the Town Mill for £170 and a meadow called Bordengates, next to the west end of West Brook bridge for £110, from Richard Morell of Polhampton. As the annual rent expected from Bordengates was £7, this represented a fair rate of interest. Thomas Morell also owned 52 acres of land in the South Field, 10 acres in Wolversdene and the rest on Bere Hill, all of which the Corporation bought in 1618 for £166, expecting an annual income of £10—a 6% return. When the Chamberlain for Charitable Uses came to reckon up, he found that £446 had been invested in property as specified above, and £184 had been lent at interest making a total of £630, which was £90 less than the £720 given to the Corporation since 1571. The real significance of the 'Vindication', for such is the title of the document prepared by the Chamberlain, is the revelation of an honest and conscientious attempt to assess the degree of mismanagement.

Before leaving the subject of mismanagement, it would be as well to turn to the Spittle almshouses. The Charity Commissioners in 1825 could not account for the origin of this charity. The houses, originally built some time before 1570 when they are first mentioned, were rebuilt in 1649 and entirely rebuilt in 1692 for four widows on land in Salisbury Road. When Bishop Crawley listed the hospitals, almshouses and free schools in the County of Southampton in 1686, he added a note that 'several ancient people can remember where there were seven score acres of land for the maintenance of the poor of that house (i.e. Spittle Almshouses), but now there is noe allowance'. If the almshouses were the successors of St Mary's Hospital then the 140 acres may have been the endowment land of that institution.

It would be wrong, however, to conclude that all gifts to the Corporation were bound to be mismanaged. There were a number of smaller legacies which were probably never intended to last for long. When Maude Hanson left 20/- to the poor of Andover in her will made and proved in 1569–70, she probably expected it to be given in individual coins to individual poor. In 1610 Thomas Cornelius left £20; in 1625 Walter Waite gave 20/- annually to the poor on the anniversary of his death 9 September, though as in 1618 he held £5 of Cornelius' gift, £13-15-0 interest for several years on £50, and a further £10 for 4 years interest on the £50 lent to Mr Bushell, it may be only his way of paying off his debt.

The major benefactor of the seventeenth century was the newcomer John Pollen. In 1702 he transferred to three trustees, the Warden of Winchester College, the Vicar and the Bailiff of Andover, the whole of Sotwell's or Seymour's Farm for the maintenance of the almshouse he had erected in 1686 in Dogpole Street on a small piece of land which was part of the waste land of the Parsonage farm. The almshouse is noted by Bishop Crawley as the 'Blew Almshouse' because the six poormen who inhabited the houses were to be provided with 2/- weekly and a blue gown annually. This and the obligation to keep the almshouses in repair means that Sotwell's Farm had an annual profit of more than £30.

One large donation of the seventeenth century seems to have been lost. An entry in the minute book for 30 August 1667 records an unanswered 'enquiry as to who holds £100 left to the poor of the town by Mr Jayes of Reading'. On the other hand, Francis Powlett's legacy (1679) of £100 remained with his family, the interest only being paid to the Corporation and usually spent in apprenticing orphans. The problem of orphan children is one which the Corporation tended to shrug off, and one device was to find a tradesman willing to take an apprentice whom he would have to clothe, feed, lodge and train for seven years. An inducement of cash helped to find such tradesmen. Three years' interest from Mr Powlett was used on 16 December 1734, £4 to James Ealls for taking Charles Fuller, £4 to James Hall for taking James Holdip, £4 to Roger Cannon for taking Peter Talmage, £2 to Richard Goddard for taking John Francis without indentures, and £1 for making three indentures. On 30 November 1744, five apprenticeships were entered into—Thomas Turner to John Trigg, tailor, Ned Cooke to John Hacker, cordwainer, John Fisher to Robert Hendy, cordwainer, Thomas Lively to William Bailey, wheelwright, and Elizabeth Knowles to John Monger, saddler, each of the five masters receiving £5. Ned Cooke did not last long, and was replaced on 11 March by Giles Gilmore.

The surviving accounts of the Charity Chamberlain, which are few and far between contrast sadly with those of the Town Chamberlain which are practically complete from 1598 to 1835. Particularly significant in the context of the allegations made by William Hayward in 1692 is the care taken by Isaac Cooper for his accounts of the Charitable Uses for 1692–1694. The disappearance of the accounts for 1678–1692 tends to support the allegations and reveals a degree of carelessness if not of corruption. Between 21 December 1692 and 98 May 1694, the Charitable Chamberlain received £82-11-4 in rents and £20-5-0 for five butchers standings under the Guildhall. Out of this £102-16-4, he spent £28-6-8 in cash gifts to the poor on St Thomas' Day, Ash Wednesday and Good Friday, and £1 in Harvest Time money which he forgot to pay until long after the harvest, the Schoolmaster's salary £42-10-0, and £2-10-0 to the four widows living at the Spittle Houses, and £4 for quit-rent on the standings to the Bailiff. The remainder £19-2-8 was spent on repairs to the various buildings, for example 12/- for a load of straw for thatching the Town Mill, 1/6 for a well bucket for the Spittle Houses, and 3/- for beer for the Workmen at the Free School and the Spittle Houses. After this meticulous recording of the trivial, the gaps in the Charitable Chamberlain's accounts recur.

The Spittle Houses were rebuilt in 1795 (on a site immediately to the rear of the Floral Clock), but no charges appear for this year in the accounts. In the succeeding years, however, the Charity Chamberlain paid carpenter's and mason's bills to the amount of £81-17-0 which appear to have been paid first by the Town Chamberlain, who then claimed the amounts from his colleague. The Spittle Houses were demolished in 1902.

Mismanagement by the Corporation seems to have affected the course of charitable gifts. John Pollen's gift was to three named trustees instead of the Corporation. Later legacies were treated with greater care. The Rev Richard Widmore, rector of Lasham and an Approved Man of Andover, whose father had been Town Clerk, directed in his will, made and proved in 1764, that the residue of his estate should be devoted by his executors to three public charities. In 1774 the Court of Chancery directed that £250 of Consolidated Stock should be purchased in the names of three trustees for 'the relief of the aged and impotent poor of the parish of Andover, or for putting poor children . . . to school or binding them out apprentices, or otherwise for the benefit of the poor'. Between 1815 and 1825 the dividends on this stock provided three apprenticeships at £7 each, 53 cloaks and 44 greatcoats distributed at Christmas 1820 and in February 1825.

In addition to his almshouses, John Pollen also left a house and garden in Dogpole Street by his will dated 1718 and proved 1719, together with an annual sum of £10 to be paid by the tenant of Marsh Court Farm, Kings Somborne, so that a schoolmistress could live in the house and teach twenty young poor children of Andover to read. John Pollen's descendants continued to interest themselves in the school, nominating the children for tuition and keeping the school-house in repair.

In 1835 the old Corporation was succeeded by the new Municipal Borough, and in the following year, the control of the Charities in Andover was vested in a new body called the Charity Trustees. The ten trustees met on 23 May 1837 and found that they were in debt. There was a balance due from the last Chamberlain of £1-3-6; but bills for £14-7-1, taxes due for £4-5-6, £4 quit-rents to the Mayor, £20 due to the Schoolmaster, and a further £24-9-0 to be paid for bread and in alms. In addition the Vicar of Andover brought a bill for £52 for proceedings in Chancery for the appointment of the Charity Trustees.

It was some time before the Trustees recovered, but careful management of their income enabled them to open an account in 1856 at the Andover Savings Bank with an initial deposit of £200. The Trustees were ultimately responsible to a national body, the Charity Commissioners, but there was still a degree of casualness, for in 1873 it was found that their accounts had not been sent to London since 1869. The Charity Trustees were admonished by the Commissioners in 1860 for investing money (at that time £400) in a local bank, and castigated for wastefulness in continuing to distribute cash benefits in sixpences.

To recover from a debt of over £100 in 1836 to a surplus of £297-3-$7\frac{1}{2}$ in 1856 argues a careful husbanding of resources. The Trustees could rely upon rents from the Town Mill and Bengers Mead, Borden Gates Meadow, 70 acres on Andover Down instead of Morell's 52 acres, Common Acre, Sottwell's Farm, property on the corner of Winchester Street which held the Town Barn and two houses, all described as near the Three Choughs, together with dividends from Widmore's Trust, and possibly fees from boarders at the Free School.

At the same time they were responsible for the Spittle Almshouses, the Acre Almshouses, the Blue or Pollen's Almshouses, and the Free Grammar School. They paid the Schoolmaster's salary, a contribution to the Vicar's salary for the Kemis lecture, weekly stipends to the tenants of the almshouses, and occasional distributions of sixpences and bread.

A new scheme was established by order of the Charity Commissioners on 17 July 1906 when the Free School had been transferred to a new Board of Governors. Most of the ancient gifts, Kemis', Cornelius', and several others together with the proceeds of the sale of the Spittle Almshouses site, were consolidated into one fund for the Acre Almshouses where four widows lived, and for pensions to other aged residents of 4/- per week. Other charitable gifts, like Widmore's, could be used at the discretion of the Trustees.

There had been a number of such gifts in the course of the nineteenth century. Ambrose Massey left by will in 1843, the sum of £300 of Consolidated Stock to be administered by the Charity Trustees. Not everyone trusted the Trustees. In 1845 the Rev William Goddard left nearly £900 to the Vicar and Mayor, and the dividends were usually distributed in coals, as were the dividends of

Miss Elizabeth Etwall's £390 of Consolidated Stock (to the poor of New Street) on or about 11 October yearly, and the dividends of £658 Consolidated left by William Safe in 1898 to the Vicar and Churchwardens.

Some legacies specified blankets or articles in kind as the needs of the poor. Martha Gale, bequeathed by her will which was proved in 1862, a legacy of £900 Consolidated Stock, the dividends of which were to be applied by the Vicar and the Mayor in the purchase of blankets to be distributed on or about St John the Evangelist's Day. In 1905 this came to sixty blankets and thirty two half crowns for thirty two lucky pensioners. The Vicar was entrusted with the dividends of £2,000 Consols given in 1869 by Rev C. H. Ridding, for the relief of the poor in kind.

The Vicar and Churchwardens were also made trustees of a legacy from the same Rev W. S. Goddard for the preservation and repair of the church which he had given to Andover. The proceeds of the sale of two houses and some land are held by the Official Trustees for the same purpose, and they also hold a fund which provides the salary of the organist and for repairs to the organ.

The Charity situation in Andover is complicated because of the size and number of the legacies. In the villages north of the town, which are included in the Borough, the situation is much simpler. David Dewar, one time Lord of the Manor of Knights Enham endowed a school and left a legacy for the poor. As a result of a Chancery case, Dewar v. Maitland, £1,716 Consols were divided between a 'teacher's salary account' paid to the school at Smannell, and a 'poor' account, the income from which was duly applied by the Rector in meat, drink and clothing to the necessitous poor. The Official Trustees are charged with distributing in fuel and clothing to the poor of Knights Enham, Little London, Woodhouse and Smannell, the dividends of the legacy of Lt Col W. H. Earle in 1887 which amounted to £980 of stock.

The twentieth century has seen a rationalisation of the Charity Trustees' role in Andover. The advent of the welfare state has made the relief of the poor less urgent, and the Trustees are now concerned with providing retirement homes, or old people's welfare homes rather than with cash payments or bags of coal. There is still a blanket distribution at Christmas but the best monument to the activities of the Charity Trustees in the twentieth century is the erection of some more old people's homes off Acre Path, not far from the old Almshouses of Common Acre.

Chapter Eleven
THE UNION WORKHOUSE

'And still new needs, new helps, new habits rise,
That graft benevolence on charities'

Behind a colourful screen of shrubs and trees in Junction Road is a red and white façade which now seems to be shyly hiding from the gaze of pedestrians. At one time, however, this retiring edifice was the most notorious building in England and Wales, largely due to the persistence of John Walter, owner of 'The Times'. In 1846, it was the 'Andover Bastille' a place so hated by the unemployed labourer that he would rather starve than enter its doors. As state help for the helpless, it was indeed a 'prison with a milder name, which few inhabit without dread or shame'.

State help was in the beginning full of fine intentions. The preamble to the Act of Parliament which abolished monasteries and nunneries contains suggestions which in the draft were in Henry VIII's own handwriting, for applying the results of the take over to 'almshouses for poor folk'. It was a pious hope rather than a real suggestion, but within sixty years of the ending of the monasteries legislation to solve the problem of the poor had reached the stage of being the most progressive in Europe. In 1597 Parliament decreed that four Overseers of the Poor should be chosen in Easter week in each parish by the Justices of the Peace with powers to set the able bodied poor, both young and old to work, to use contributed money to relieve those unable to work, and to erect houses for the poor on the wasteland of the manor. A consolidating Act in 1601 including the apprenticing of orphan children and power to enforce contributions for orphans from relatives. Public charity was ready if private charity should prove inadequate.

Vagabondage and vagrancy were one of the major social problems created by the economic depression of the sixteenth century. Beggars flocked to the large towns where their presence was regarded by the inhabitants with hostility. By an Act of 1547, if a person had not spent the last three years in one place, he was to be returned to the place of his birth, and all Bailiffs and Constables were empowered in that year to carry such strangers to the boundary of the Hundred and pass them on to the next Hundred until they reached the place of their birth. This could have been difficult since there were no birth certificates, and Thomas Cromwell's instruction to parish priests to keep a register of baptisms though made in 1538 was not generally obeyed. The Town Chamberlain's accounts contain several entries of this sort: 1627: 'for sending Wayt's maide with child with a horse to hurriton 2/6' and '31 July 1623 to Tho. Wigmore for the Conveyinge away A man & his wif and a childe to Salsbury after the Corte 5/-' and 1650 'Payd John Cooke for carrying a woman nere her time to Clatford 2/6'.

In 1662 the 'Legal Settlement' Statute of 1547 was revived; the Civil War had created more population movement that any earlier event; a Yorkshire surname 'Hepperby' occurs in Andover's Register of Baptisms in 1646 and belongs to Isabel, a daughter of one of Sir Thomas Fairfax' soldiers. There were exceptions to the 1662 Act; harvest workers with a certificate from a Minister or a Justice of the Peace, and workers with a certificate of settlement could continue to search for employment, since their relief was acknowledged by a parish. Casual wanderers who could not find employment and housing within forty days were liable to be sent to the plantations overseas or returned to the place of their birth.

The earliest poor rate list for the parish of Andover which has been preserved is for 1655. The list of monthly contributors is headed by William Gold the Bailiff at 2/- and continues with the names of 161 other householders and 18 landholders in Andover, 2 in Woodhouse, 6 in King's Enham and 6 in Hatherden. Between them they are to contribute £5-14-0 for one rate every month. The rate was confirmed by the Bailiff and a Justice on 26 April. Nine men did not pay, and on 27 March 1656 some articles were distrained perhaps a little unfairly. Thomas Paine, who was rated for 6d per month lost 'one Bras Morter & Pestle . . . waing 66 pounds & half a 6d the pound cometh to £1-14-9' which was nearly six years' contributions. Richard Cook and John Philpott who appraised the goods were more accurate in the case of John Seagrove who owed 2d a month. From him they took 'i Reme of Browne paper' valued at 2/- and from Robert Evred (or Evered) they took 'i hand sawe 2 Augors i goudg' valued at 2/6 for his 2d per month.

In the summer of 1655, the collectors took in £28-8-10 and spent £28-7-0. Forty eight old people were helped with cash amounts between 3/- and 30/-. Seven children were boarded and lodged.

105

Some payments were made for washing and lodging and the burial expenses, knell, shroud and grave, for two men were paid. Some clothes were purchased for the children and some payments made to the sick; and the final payment of 1/- was the very reasonable fee 'for wrightinge this account'.

The Churchwardens and Overseers of the Poor shared with modern rating authorities a desire to reduce the amount of the rates. One way was to reduce the number of children for whose maintenance the parish would be responsible. In 1626 the Town Chamberlain paid 2/6 on 19 October 'for the sending boyes to Southampton to gooe for verginie'. In normal families two parents were responsible for their children, and the parish unwillingly accepted responsibility for orphans; for one parent children the parish insisted on finding a second parent to share the cost.

Margaret Tarrant made a voluntary statement to the Justices on 9 March 1736 in which she explained that:

'she was brought to bed St Paul's Day last past . . . of a male child which is living . . . That John New who lives a servant at Kent's Mill . . . is the father, who hath carnal knowledge of her body several times, the first time in her mother's house about a month before Whitsuntide last and after that at the White Hart where she lived as a servant; That about five years ago she was married to Thomas Tarrant at Andover who left her above two years ago & she hath not seen him since; That about thirteen months ago he wrote her that he was listed a soldier & expected to go to Gibraltar every day since that she hath not heard from him . . . can't say if her husband is living or dead'.

Poor Margaret Tarrant. Some years later Henry Dickman the younger bound himself for £100 to provide for the child he had fathered on Margaret Tarrant which was born on 9 May 1743. The bond is dated 7 September 1744 when the child was sixteen months old and fairly certain to live for some time.

Typical is the case of George Humber, the subject of legal proceedings between the parishes of Andover and North Tidworth. He had lived with and worked for Anthony Yewings of North Tidworth from Michaelmas 1699 to Michaelmas 1703, and then contracted himself to John and Thomas Carter of Charlton for one year. Before the year was up he had become entangled with an unnamed female whom he had been forced to marry in June; on his wedding night he absented himself from his employers' house and for this he was dismissed. The Justices for Andover realising that the cost of supporting George Humber, his wife and child-to-be would fall upon the parish rates, and fearing that North Tidworth Overseers would claim that his dismissal was unjust, promptly sent him back to North Tidworth claiming that this was his last legal residence.

A system so fruitful of inter-community differences was clearly unsatisfactory; in Bristol in 1698, the City Council decided to create a Workhouse where the ablebodied could be housed, fed and given some useful work to do. Since most industrial processes were by hand, the idea spread quickly in other large urban centres where there was unemployment. In Andover the Churchwardens and Overseers did not decide to have a Workhouse until 1733 when they chose the 'Plough' in Winchester Street which was owned by Dorothy Baker as a suitable building. A lease of the premises was accepted at a special Vestry meeting; the rent was £5-5-0 for fourteen years with an option to purchase for £105. Three weeks earlier, the Churchwardens and Overseers had arranged with Thomas Noyes, a shalloon maker, to employ all the needy poor for the next three years in making shalloon—a kind of lining cloth.

Thomas Noyes would supply the necessary stock of wool and other material while the 'Implements and Utensils' for shalloon making would be supplied by the Churchwardens and Overseers who would also supply all the furniture and implements necessary for housing the poor in the house. Noyes would look after the building and see that the inmates were decently fed and lodged and regulated. He was to choose a matron for the workhouse and to be paid £10 per year in four instalments. His profit came from being able to purchase the work done by the inmates at 75% of the usual rates. It must have seemed a reasonable risk since Noyes agreed to pay a penal sum of £50 if he defaulted on the contract.

The agreement with Thomas Noyes was not renewed and there was a fifteen month gap before the next agreement to manage the Workhouse was signed. The new master, Richard Willis, was an apothecary and not prepared to undertake the same conditions as his predecessor. In return for providing food and drink in accordance with a prescribed bill of fare, for taking care of their clothes, for keeping the house clean, warmed and lit, and for providing suitable work on materials supplied by him, Richard Willis could in 1737 have the use of the Workhouse and implements rent free and insured free, and would receive 18d per person per week for the first two years and 15d per week for the last five years of the seven year agreement, together with five guineas towards the cost of any new building, and the necessary fuel for the Workhouse for the first year. The most important clause, however, is that which specifies that he shall not employ any servant 'in such a manner as such Servant may gain a settlement thereby in the said parish of Andover'.

Before the ending of Richard Willis' lease, the Churchwardens and Overseers had come to an agreement with Benjamin Munday, a shalloon-maker, who was not prepared to be Master, though he would provide materials and take fourpence of every shilling profit. Another shalloon-maker, William Reynolds, and his wife, Elizabeth, became Master and Mistress at a salary of £20 and their diet. The Orders and General Bill of Fare were the same as for Richard Willis. The agreement ran its full term and possibly a further two years, for the last lease is dated 13 May 1751. On this occasion, William Waters, sergeweaver and his wife are to be paid £20 in four quarterly instalments to supervise the poor of the Workhouse, 'in such Labour, Work or Business as they are respectively most apt for, or as they can respectively earn most money at'. Any profit was to be kept by the Churchwardens and Overseers, who in return paid all the costs of running the Workhouse.

Nothing more is known about this Workhouse; it may have been allowed to run down by the Churchwardens and Overseers, for the Corporation decided on 7 November 1775 to oppose the scheme for setting up County Workhouses which had been proposed in the last session of Parliament. They felt that the proposal would 'not answer the good ends proposed but will be cruel to the poor and add rather than diminish the expense of their support'. Lack of any information about the Workhouse or about payments to the poor in Andover in the period 1770–1835 leads to fruitless speculation.

Pauperization was by this time a national problem; what had been the most advanced system in 1601 was now obsolete. The problem of the poor was exacerbated by the rise in the cost of living due to the Napoleonic Wars and aggravated by the period of economic distress which followed. The passing of the Poor Law Amendment Act of 1835 forced urban and rural parishes to join together, sometimes unwillingly as may be deduced from the letter of the Assistant Commissioner charged with the task of forming the Andover Union. In the final paragraph of that letter dated Andover, 15 June 1835, Colonel C. A. a'Court wrote 'Hereafter I propose to send to the Board merely an analysis of my notes in the several Parishes I may inspect. The notes themselves I cannot get on without. They stood me in excellent stead today and enabled me at once to silence incipient opposition'.

Whence came this 'incipient opposition'? Was it from the outlying parishes who foresaw difficulties for the poor who might be forced to travel long distances? Was it from Andover itself, where the delegates knowing the uselessness of the previous Workhouse attempted to point out the stupidity of competing against machines? Or was it that mutual antipathy between town and country? Whichever it was, Colonel a'Court overcame it and in Bishops Court Lane in 1836 the Board of Guardians for the Andover Union built a Union Workhouse to the plans of the Commissioners' architect Sampson Kempthorne. As might have been foreseen the Board found great difficulty in providing suitable work for the inmates. After all, if there had been enough agricultural work in the surrounding countryside, there would have been no one in the Workhouse. The Guardians' solution, grinding bones for fertiliser, combined with deficiencies in diet and manipulation of accounts led to the great 'Andover Scandal' of 1846. Mr Punch wrote verses about it; 'The Times' thundered, but Peel's government was already falling. The result was two enormous volumes of a Parliamentary Select Committee which contain some wonderful details of agricultural life in the 1840s and show just how degrading a Workhouse could be, and how careless amateur administrators are. The one important result was that the Poor Law Commissioners became answerable to the House of Commons for the deeds committed by the Guardians.

No doubt the gruesome gnawing of rotten marrow, the face scarring splintering of pounded bones, the atrocious treatment of unfortunate women, the vicious behaviour of the Master and the Matron, ex-Sergeant Major McDougal and his wife, could be parallelled in other institutions, and indeed McDougal's successor was dismissed for scandalous behaviour, though with less publicity. How far the stand taken by Hugh Munday against the establishment as represented by his fellow guardians was due to personal pique and how far to humanitarian beliefs and innate courage demands a special study. Certainly the later history of the Andover Union Workhouse is less notorious; the inmates seem to have suffered in times of stress and severe unemployment, but to have become less so as public opinion ameliorated the original principle of 'less eligibility' which ensured that however hard life was outside, it was always harder inside.

The Poor Law, and the Union Workhouse ended in 1929 to be replaced by other forms of relief for those in need. The Workhouse building remained and continues to perform a useful service, being St John's Hospital for the aged and handicapped.

Chapter Twelve
THE TOWN BRIDGE

'Nay troth, th'Apostles (tho' perhaps too rough)
Had once a pretty gift of Tongues enough:
Yet these were all poor Gentlemen! I dare
Affirm, 'twas Travel made them what they were.'

Crossed and re-crossed by thousands every day the Town Bridge does not betray its presence by a narrowing of the highway, nor by a steepening of gradients on either side. Indeed, it is a barely noticeable feature spanning a shallow watercourse, which dives between concrete banks as though trying to deny the presence of fish: yet, insignificant though it may seem, it was once the essential component in the communications network of the area. Its existence is a comparatively modern feature. The Harroway, of which much mention has already been made, crossed the river by a ford. Until quite recently carts were driven down the yard by the 'Bell' from the High Street to the stream, where the horses cooled their hocks and gently lapped the alkaline water while their drivers cleaned and washed the cart, a pleasant and idyllic scene.

The earliest record of a bridge occurs in the Town Chamberlains' Accounts for 1513–18, and the item, the repair of Westbridge, suggests the existence of two bridges. Round about 1610, the Town Chamberlains laid out 5/- 'for making the littell brigge going to the spetell', which also implies the existence of a great or town bridge. It is very probable that both bridges were fit only for pedestrians or horsemen. The payment of 4/7d in 1598 for a 'plank to make the way against Weyhill', may be an earlier repair, but in any case suggests a weight limit.

It was as a point on the east-west road that Andover was best known. The Plantagenet Kings did and the Norman Kings may have stopped at Andover on their progresses around England. Letters written by Henry III and Edward I dated at Andover are part of the national history. But Andover seems to have been a turning point in many potentially dangerous moments. It was along the Salisbury Road that the supporters of Protector Somerset were marching in 1549. Their nerve failed as they approached Andover, and instead of continuing to London they returned to Wilton and wrote to the

Protector to tell him they had changed their minds. It was also from Salisbury that Charles I approached Andover in 1644, on his way to London, from which purpose he may have been deflected by the little skirmish towards evening between his vanguard and some of Sir William Waller's rearguard, which is grandiloquently referred to as the 'Battle of Andover'. It was in the reverse direction from Newbury to Salisbury that Sir Thomas Fairfax' army moved in 1645 to quell the west; some deserters were hung on a gallows at the western boundary of the town at Red Post Bridge. Pursuing the mutinous Levellers, Oliver Cromwell stopped long enough in Andover on 12 May 1649 to deliver a speech to his three regiments.

It was in greater haste that King James II came in 1688. In the evening of 25 October he wrote, from Andover, an appeal for help to Lord Dartmouth. His vain attempt to stem the advance of William of Orange and the Protestants came to an end when his son-in-law, Prince George of Denmark, and his young Irish supporter, the Duke of Ormonde, deserted him that night. James II returned to London, but William III avoided Andover, taking a more northerly route through the Kennet Valley and Newbury.

Not all royal movements were so belligerent. James I passed through Andover several times on his journeys. The Town Chamberlains' accounts are scattered with payments to the 'king's gentlemen' and the 'king's trumpeters'. At a much later stage George III spent one night at the Star and Garter on his return from Weymouth. Whether Queen Elizabeth I ever visited the town is not certain. None of her known progresses seems to have passed near enough to cause her to stop even though in her 'Great Charter of 1599' she described Andover as 'an ancient and populous Town and Thoroughfare through our whole Kingdom of England into the Western Parts'.

During the Middle Ages the Church played a dual role by encouraging people to travel as pilgrims, and by keeping the bridges in repair to make such travel possible. It also provided hostels for travellers. One such was the Hospital of St John the Baptist situated at the northern end of New Street. Here, a warden and brothers and sisters who were aged but not infirm, served the travellers' needs as far as they could in the Hospital. Religious services were held in a chapel on the other side of the Pilgrims' Way, where the priest was paid and appointed by the Gild Merchant of Andover. A vineyard behind the Hospital completed the religious foundation which catered principally for pilgrims to and from Canterbury, but also for merchants and other travellers.

The Reformation changed this. St John's Hospital was taken over

111

by the Corporation in 1552, and leased the following year to Thomas Reve, a mercer. Another Thomas Reve, also a mercer, was the tenant of St John's House in a lease dated 1620, and from 1660 to 1825 there is an almost complete set of profitable leases by the Corporation; St John's House and the lands with which it had been endowed constituted a large proportion of the Corporation's rentable property.

Travellers after 1553 were therefore compelled to use the inns, of which the 'Angel' is the oldest remaining. It was built in 1444–46, the carpenters' contract for the construction being still in the possession of the then owners, the Warden, Fellows and Scholars of the College of St Mary, Winchester. Although the position of the various parts of the inn were specified in the contract, the builders, John Harding and Richard Holnerst were allowed to alter the details. As a result, the north wing, the part which is now used, was the stable block approached through the archway so placed as to face the London Road. Much of the east, as well as the south and west wings of the courtyard have now disappeared but the archway in the east wing remains. An inventory of 1632 lists 26 living rooms in the Inn with fascinating names like 'Unicorn Chamber', 'Half Moon Chamber' and Fawlcon Chamber'; the innkeeper, Richard Pope, was the ancestor of the poet, Alexander Pope, from whose works are taken the quotations which head each chapter of this book.

Among other inns which may have been used by travellers was the 'Bell' in the High Street, on a site now covered by Woolworths. It was first built in 1451 and then transferred by Bishop Wayneflete in 1481 to Magdalen College, Oxford. The property, which extended from the Market Place to the river bank, was redeveloped by the College in 1534. Nicholas Langridge, a Fellow of the College, was appointed to oversee the work, and his record-book has been preserved. It reveals remarkable sophistication in building technique and organisation. Starting in March, Langridge purchased the trees and arranged for them to be sawn to the correct sizes, and at the same time arranged for a supply of lime and bricks. The site was cleared in May and June, and the foundations laid in July, by which time all the necessary timber had been assembled. The framework was finished quickly, though details like doors were not completed until November. The ironwork was started in July, the tiling was done between August and October, the glazing in October, and the paintings of the finished building in November. This last operation took nearly four weeks and used 15 lb of red lead, $1\frac{1}{2}$ pints of oil, 59 lbs of 'yellow ochre' and size made from $1\frac{1}{2}$ bushels of leather.

The maintenance of the roads and bridges collapsed with the Reformation. The parish authorities were regarded by Parliament as the logical successors. An Act of 1555 laid the duty of repairing roads and bridges upon the parish. Surveyors of Highways, either four or two, were to be appointed to allocate the tasks of collecting suitable repair material, carting it to the appropriate places, and filling in the holes or ruts. Four days labour was expected from each parishioner, and those with carts were expected to lend them for the occasion.

But the power of the unpaid Surveyors was in practice limited by the willingness of their neighbours. What survives is not a record of what was done, but lists of men who refused to help either by lending their horses and carts, or by refusing to perform the statute labour required. The post of Surveyor of the Highways was not sought by everyone and sometimes the Surveyors were charged with not trying.

In Andover the work was shared by the Corporation and the Surveyors of the Highways. The Town Chamberlains' Accounts contain references to payments for work done. The earliest is '6 April 1627, paid Bugley, pavior, for paving in the stratt as appeareth per his note the som of £1-14-8'. Later in the same year R. Hopgood was paid 5/- for 'stones and car. to the mending London way'. After 1656 payments became more frequent; '11 June 1656 to Robert Piper and Dawkins for the highways 6/8', '6 June 1657 paid Wm Barwick for the highways 10/-'. Perhaps these entries represent the Corporation's debt to the Surveyors, a suggestion strengthened by the direct payment in 1804–5 of £1.10.0 by the Corporation.

The Corporation seem to have assumed responsibility for the 'town bridge'. One early entry is '30 January 1621 payed Mr Rich. Pope Baylife for the repayre of the Town Bridge £7'. Smaller amounts were paid in 1650 and 1658, and similar payments in 1663, 1664 and 1665 suggest that the rainfall was considerably higher than normal during this time. This resulted in occasional flooding and a heavy accumulation of rubbish against the piers of the bridge which needed 'scowring' 'drawing' or 'riding'. The Town Bridge was clearly the responsibility of the Town of Andover, and because of this, Andover was exempted from contributing to the upkeep of County Bridges like Redbridge, Christchurch Bridge and Boldre Bridge.

If the County Justices did not interfere in the Town Bridge, they did take note of the highways round Andover, though oddly enough the first mention of these roads in the records of the County Bench is a complaint by the Constables of the Borough of Andover in 1649.

The burden of their complaint was that travellers were evading the orders of the recent Act of Parliament forbidding travel on the Lord's Day, by using roads through adjoining parishes. The County Justices obliged by issuing an order to these parishes 'to keep true and diligent ward' to see that the Act was obeyed. In Andover the Hundred Court oversaw the state of the highways and indicates sometimes, the persons responsible for its repair. Sometimes the County Justices made comments. In 1693, the 5th year of William and Mary, Edward Pyle of Wallop 'one of Their Majesties Justices of the Peace', did 'present upon his owne view the highway leading from Andover to Little Ann, which ought to be repaired by the Inhabitants of Andover before the next session upon paine of £10.' Four years later, he wrote a friendly note to the Town Clerk of Andover pointing out that he had previously complained about the state of the roads in Andover particularly the one which he took from Wallop to Hurstbourne: if the Corporation would promise to do something about repairing it, he would not mention it at the next Quarter Sessions which he would attend by way of Andover and Hurstbourne. 'Indeed, I write this as a timely prevention of a misunderstanding between my good friends of Andover and your old friend and servant, E. Pyle' he concluded.

The task of the Surveyors of Highways became more burdensome as pack-horse traffic gave way to horse-drawn traffic. The notice of appointment as Surveyors of the Highways for 1734 of Joseph Bunny the younger, John Forster, William Gilbert and William Clark survives. After reciting their duties according to the Acts of 1691, 1715 and 1733, it concludes with a list of the regulations about waggons and carts for hire and otherwise. Waggons travelling for hire must not be drawn by 'more than six horses, either at length, or in pairs, or sideways', and carts for hire must not have more than three horses. Any extra horse may be seized and claimed from a Justice by the person seizing it. The same may happen if a Waggon 'having the Wheels bound with Streaks, or Tire of a less Breath than two Inches and a half when worn, or being set on with Rose-headed Nails' is drawn by more than three horses. Regulations like these were designed to preserve the roads from too much wear, but they did not apply to 'Waggons or Carts employed in Husbandry or Manuring of Land, or in Carrying of Cheese, Butter, Hay, Straw, Corn unthrashed, Coals, Chalk, or any one Tree or Piece of Timber, or any one Stone or Block of Marble, Caravans and cover'd Carriages of Noblemen and Gentlemen for their private Use, or Timber, Ammunition or Artillery for His Majesty's Service'.

The alternative to the system of statute labour by the parish was a Turnpike Trust. This was a way of raising money for the maintenance of the road from those who used it. Contributions, fixed by regulations, were collected at turnpikes or toll-gates which the Trustees were empowered to erect to control the traffic using the repaired road. The advantages of the Turnpike Trust were obvious where a number of parishes and counties were responsible for a long stretch of road. On the great North Road, only the Doncaster-Retford section was not under a Turnpike Trust by 1750. By this same date, the whole of the London-Bath and Bristol Road had been turnpiked as had the roads from London to Shrewsbury, London to Chester, London to Portsmouth, London to Canterbury and London to Harwich. The Salisbury and Exeter Road from London was still not modernised by 1750.

One cannot be sure that the Corporation took the lead in setting up a Turnpike Trust, but a minute made on 14 January 1755 notes that members agreed to petition the House of Commons for a Turnpike Road 'from Basingstoke' thro' Wortin, Overton, Whitchurch, Hursborn Pryors, Andover and Middle Wallop to Lobcomb Corner'. The resulting Trust became known as the 'Andover Turnpike Trust' and added several branch roads to its original line.

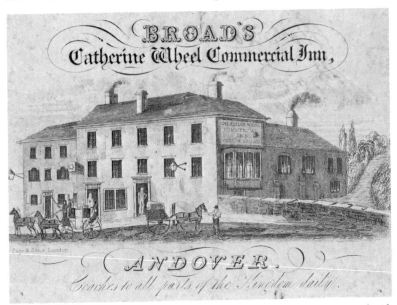

Billhead, 1835. The building, with a remodelled front, still stands in Bridge Street beside the river. The subscript reads 'Coaches to all parts of the Kingdom daily'.

The Corporation in 1755 cannot have realised the effect that increased traffic would have on the Town Bridge. Less than four years after their petition, the Corporation met on 8 December 1758 and, considering the amount of damage, ordered the erection of a 'Bar and Lamp' to stop wheeled traffic. Coaches and waggons were expected to use the ford, while pedestrians and horsemen could cross the bridge. At the same meeting the Corporation gave notice to the Turnpike Trustees to make good the damage done at the lower end of Brick-kiln Street and White Hart corner. The re-entrant angle at the south end of the present Star and Garter, then called the White Hart, was created in order to widen the carriageway and enable coaches to negotiate the corner.

In 1762 a proposal was put forward for a new Winchester-Andover turnpike and on 12 June 1764 the Corporation agreed to lend money to the Trustees against repayment of interest from the tolls. The first interest received, namely £5 in 1766, was put towards the payment of apprenticeships. On 14 May 1766, the Corporation decided to support the proposed Newbury Turnpike Trust against opposition, and were prepared to encourage this project with cash. Twelve days later they recorded their thanks to their M.P., Sir John Griffin Griffin, 'for great labours in obtaining the Act for the Turnpike from Hursley to Newbury'. Interest on the money lent to the Winchester Trust was still being paid to the Corporation in 1770.

The Turnpike Trusts meant an increase in wheeled traffic particularly coaches. A number of these coaches, for Salisbury, Exeter, or Weymouth stopped in Andover, but the longest run was that of the 'Quicksilver' or Devonport Royal Mail for Plymouth. This left St Martins le Grand in London at 8.0 p.m. and passed through Andover (67 miles) at 2.20 a.m. reaching Devonport (216 miles) at 5.14 p.m., an average speed of 10 m.p.h. Passengers then crossed by ferry and reached Falmouth at 1.5 a.m., less than 30 hours after leaving London. (It was while waiting at the White Hart in Whitchurch in December 1832 for the Quicksilver that John Henry Newman composed the hymn 'Lead, kindly light'). In addition two interesting bills survive. John Richard Birnie (successor to Charles Foyle) ran a fly-wagon twice a week from Andover to the Angel Inn, Fleet Market, London: he charged George Thompson 16/2 for carrying 4 cwts of furniture which had come by barge to Basing-stoke. Thomas Russell & Co. who also ran fly-wagons to London charged Thompson £4.1.2. for carrying 18 cwt in 4 cases, but this sum included 1/- for 'men to drink'.

There may have been a feeling in Andover that there had been unnecessary delay in adopting the Turnpike Trust system. Some were early advocates of another form of transport, the canal. They pointed out the ease with which corn, now being produced in large quantities as a result of the increased amount of arable land, could be sold at Andover and shipped by barge to the coast, rather than send it to be sold at Newbury for shipment down the Kennet and Thames. Local patriotism conquered economic sense and a canal was built from Andover to Redbridge near Southampton. Most of the money to build the canal came from Andover and the surrounding villages. The results did not meet the expectations of the investors, but there were compensations. Coal became relatively cheap. Chance has preserved a bill from 1835 showing that T. & W. H. Heath (of the banking and brewing family) were selling Newcastle coals from the Canal wharf at 14d per bushel.

As the amount of transport to and from Andover increased, it became necessary to improve the internal roads, which the Corporation as a Corporation were not concerned with. Individual members of the Corporation with members of the Heath family and William S. Wakeford, the banker, twenty-three in all, wrote to the Bailiff on 29 July 1814 asking him to call a meeting to consider the 'expediency of applying to Parliament in the next session to obtain an Act for Paving, Lighting, Watching and Cleansing the Borough'. Ralph Etwall, the Bailiff, called the meeting on 15 August, and within a year an Act had been obtained. Because, as the Act put it, 'the Foot-Ways of the Streets, Lanes, and other public Passages and Places . . . are in general much out of repair and very inconvenient', the Bailiff, the Corporation, the Vicar and 62 named gentlemen are appointed Pavement Commissioners, with power to raise a rate on every property within three-quarters of a mile from the Guildhall, measured by the nearest Public Highway. The money so collected could be used to pay interest charges and repayments on a larger sum spent on paving and other public utilities.

The Pavement Commissioners wasted little time. The Act was passed in 1815, the first meeting of the Commissioners was held on 29 May, and after due notice, by publication in the 'Salisbury Times', 'Hampshire Chronicle', 'Portsmouth Telegraph', and 'The Times' newspapers, a meeting was held to consider tenders on 22 December at the Star and Garter. A contract was arranged on 8 April 1816 between the Commissioners and William Ellis of Portsea, pavier, and John Windover of Andover, stonemason, for paving the streets as directed by the Commissioners beginning on 10 April and ending before 29 September 1818 'unless some obstructions shall happen in and to the Andover Canal Navigation so as to prevent the Passage of Boats or Barges laden with Stone' at fixed prices ranging from 9/6 a yard for 'Purbec horse pitchers' not less than 6 to 8 inches in depth, to 8d per square yard for pitching with flint or other stone provided by the Commissioners.

The money for this operation was raised by granting an annuity of £63 to Catherine Jacob of Monxton in return for £700, an annuity of £17 to John Reeves of Andover, grocer, in return for £200, and a £30 annuity to Henrietta Eaton of Andover for £300. On 4 July 1821 The Commissioners made a further contract with John Windover and his son John, now described as paviers, for similar work at similar prices. Purbeck Horse Pitchers were reduced to 9/2d, but Guernsey Squares (for the crossings) remained 9/3d a square yard, and the rate for paving with 'Purbeck common size Flatners, laid in chalk lime Mortar not less than 7 inches square' was 8d per foot.

Lighting the Borough was rather more complicated but the Canal was a potent factor in the solution. In 1838, the Corporation, the Pavement Commissioners, five Trustees of the Andover Turnpike and the Surveyors of the Highways for Andover, came to an agreement with William Morley Stears, of Stroud, Gloucestershire, a Gas Engineer, for the erection of Gas works on land next to the Canal. Here barges could unload coal conveniently for the retorts and stills which refined the gas and stored it in a holder. The Andover Gas Light and Coke Company remained a private company until taken over by the Corporation in 1903, so the supply of coal gas for lighting the town became a matter for negotation between the Company and the Borough Council acting for the Pavement Commissioners. There were long discussions as to the price of the supply, and sometimes arguments about the placing of gas-lamps, especially one outside the Guildhall.

Watching the streets of the Borough at night was one of the duties which was originally shared amongst the householders and supervised by the constables. Occasionally offenders were noted and fined but in time the practice lapsed. The Pavement Act made little difference to this situation; no record remains of any night-watchman being specially appointed, and it is likely that the duty was left to the local constables especially after these had been appointed by the Town Council.

Such was the position in 1840; a town with some paved streets, some street lighting, a well-organised system of coaches and wagons and a posting-master, John Woodward who was appointed to the establishment of Her Majesty's Stables by the Earl of Albemarle in

1839. A new form of transport was becoming popular in other areas of the Kingdom and one would have expected the people of Andover to exert themselves in the matter of a railway just as they had in the case of the Turnpike Trusts and the Canal. Unfortunately, Andover lay in disputed territory where the Great Western Railway, wanting a route to Southampton, clashed with the London and South Western Railway, wanting a route to Bristol. The result was that from 1840 to 1855 the nearest station to Andover was Andover Road, eleven miles away at Micheldever. The existing Gallicar Way was taken over by the Andover Turnpike Trust in 1840 and lowered by cutting through the chalk at the top of Bere Hill. It is ironic that the railway was the cause of one of the last Turnpiked roads in Andover.

Attempts were made to bring a railway to Andover. In 1845 there was a proposal to link Andover with Didcot on the Great Western system, and another to link Andover with Southampton. In 1846 came a grander proposal to make a Manchester and Southampton Railway through Andover, and another Andover and Southampton Junction Railway. In 1847, an Andover-Cheltenham railway was proposed but none of these five schemes progressed beyond planning. In the meantime Salisbury was already connected by rail to London through Southampton, so a Basingstoke–Salisbury link would provide a more direct route. Plans were submitted in 1851 and again in 1852, and the railway—a single track—finally arrived in Andover in 1855.

With one line already running through the northern outskirts of the town, feeder lines became easier to contemplate as the rival planners busied themselves. In 1859 an Andover–Redbridge Railway was proposed; in 1860 an Andover–Redbridge extension to Southampton; in 1861 plans were deposited for an Andover–Redbridge and Southampton Railway, as well as for an Andover and Redbridge Railway, an Andover and Great Western Railway, and an Andover and Redbridge Junction Railway branch of the L. & S.W.R. More plans were deposited in 1862 and 1863, and a single track from Andover to Southampton was completed in 1865.

Other interesting plans which came to nothing were an Andover, Radstock and Bristol Railway (1865) and an Upavon and Andover Railway, a petition for which was approved by the Borough Council in 1866. An Andover Newbury and Didcot line was suggested in 1872. More serious ideas were revivals of the Manchester Southampton project; within a fortnight in 1873 two Railway Acts were passed, one authorising a line from Swindon through Marlborough to Andover, thus enabling South Wales to send coal direct to

Southampton, and the other authorising a line from Didcot through Newbury and Whitchurch to Southampton, thus making a direct link with Manchester. Neither project made much progress at first. The S.M. & A. opened the section to Andover in 1882, while the D.N. & S. did not open between Didcot and Winchester until 1885. In the meantime, the L. & S.W. (or the Long, Slow and Weary) Railway had opened a picturesque branch from Fullerton Junction on the Andover–Redbridge line to Hurstbourne on the main line thus making an alternative route and rendering the D.N. & S. superfluous as far as passengers from Whitchurch to Southampton were concerned. This was not the end of ideas. As late as 1902 the possibility of a railway link between Bristol and Basingstoke through Wildhern and Enham was being discussed.

The rails from Southampton had been laid partly over the bed of the canal which had been filled with chalk from quarries along the hillside between Fullerton and Stockbridge; these are sometimes referred to as the 'canal's gravestones'. Andover Town Station was built upon land which had been the canal wharf area (and the pig market) and the connection with Andover Junction station was made over the area drained by the West brook. In place of the 'littel bridge' of 1606 was a level crossing which proved to be a great nuisance. Soon after its construction, the meetings of the Town Council frequently minuted complaints about the design of the 'cuckoo-pens', by which pedestrians crossed the rails. The controversy raged from 1869 to 1885 and included a public outcry in 1878 about the closure of the gates while shunting and loading operations were carried on at the Town Station, which went so far as to threaten a complaint to the Board of Trade.

In the meantime the S.M. & A., renamed Midland and South Western Junction, had been made into a profitable railway. When the outbreak of the South African War in 1899 stimulated the War Office into building activity at Tidworth, the Tidworth Camp Railway—a Government owned branch line—from Ludgershall, became more important than the main M. & S.W.J. line. Receipts from Tidworth exceeded those from all other stations on the line combined. During the Second World War, the M. & S.W.J., like its rival the D.N. & S., became essential arteries for the D-Day build-up. Along these distinctly rural rails were transported much of the military might of the Allied Armies, a use which could not have been envisaged by the original promoters. In fact the D.N. & S. owed its existence to an agricultural recession, the local landowners arguing that a railway would open new markets for the produce of their

Map for Salisbury Plain Manoeuvres, 1910.

tenants' work, and would thus stimulate the tenants to increase production and so be able to pay their rents.

Such considerations, however, did not affect the people of Andover. They were no doubt pleased to be able to travel rapidly east, west, north and south, and Bishop's Court Lane was renamed prosaically Junction Road. They became used to the Midland Red engines hauling red coaches up and down the track behind the houses in Junction Road, and crossing Bridge Street on their way to and from Andover Town Station. At the same time at Andover Junction Station were the chocolate and brass engines of the L. & S.W. with salmon and brown carriages, and express passenger trains were at their most visible glory crossing the embankment which limited the northern expansion of the town. Not that railway traffic was always free-flowing. The great snowstorm of January 1881 caused great delay in the cuttings between Salisbury, Andover and Basingstoke. The train from Exeter was already an hour late at Salisbury, and became even later, for the snow drifts were so thick that they caked up the ashpan of the locomotive and prevented any draught from reaching the fire. Eventually the train proceeded to Basingstoke in bursts of about 300 yards, for Jack Rendall, the driver, unhooked the coaches and then rammed the snowdrift until lack of draught caused him to stop, clear the ashpan, raise steam, return to the coaches and pull them the distance cleared.

One important result of the railways was the introduction of a standard or 'railway' time which was the same for all towns. On the wall of a firm of estate agents in London Street is a sundial which records the difference between London time and Andover time. General Shubrick in 1854 presented a large reliable clock to the Andover Trust which was placed on the wall of the Tollgate house at the top of Western Road, since the Church and the Market House (Town Hall) were already equipped. The ending of the Trust in 1872 presented the Trustees with the problem of disposal. The roads were taken over by the County or the Urban Sanitary Authorities and the office of Surveyor of the Highways ended on 11 April 1874. The clock was returned to the Council who were at a loss until the Trustees of the Mechanics Institute offered to pay for its removal and installation in the wall of the Institute next to the Town Bridge. The Winchester and Newbury Turnpikes were not dis-turnpiked until 1880 though the Council had taken over the functions of the Surveyors of the Highways in 1874 and the Paving Commissioners in 1876.

Its new responsibilities for the streets of Andover created

The Andover Railcrash, 1914.

problems for the Town Council. Appointing a Surveyor was comparatively easy; so was dividing the roads into areas, but persuading contractors to deliver materials at reasonable rates was more difficult. When the materials were delivered and spread, a steam roller had to be hired (at 27/6 a day including driver) and since the roads were not tarred, they had to be watered to keep the dust down. Watercarts sprung leaks and had to be repaired. Meantime the pavements needed attention, and pedestrians were reluctant to walk on the new Val de Travers asphalt instead of the good, old-fashioned stone slabs. Finally the protesters were persuaded in 1877 and thereafter asphalt was used for pavements. Much later it was actually used on the road because the new rubber tyres tended to suck the dust from between the cracks where the iron tyres of the waggons had consolidated the stone surface.

The level crossing in the town itself became a more serious hindrance as motor traffic increased. By 1960 the use of the A303 as the London–Penzance Trunk Road had led to increased frustration whenever the crossing had to be closed. On some occasions traffic built up in mile-long queues completely blocking the flow of traffic. Indeed any accident in the narrow streets resulted in long waits for those whose business took them through Andover. A by-pass had been needed and was planned for many years before it was built, and the delay was partly because of uncertainty about the future of Andover. The action of the Greater London Council and the Hampshire County Council in agreeing to the planned expansion of Andover gave an opportunity to rethink the road system around Andover in new terms. The result was an inner ring road circling the town centre, linked to an outer ring road, of which the southern section would serve as a by-pass for the whole area, and the northern section, servicing the new industrial areas, would be a Spine Road for the whole structure. The first sections of the Spine Road, replacing the vagaries of 'Drunken Tree Drove' with a smoothly graded and inclined surface was begun in 1965, and the by-pass completed in 1969.

The first omnibuses had made their appearance in Andover in 1929. Like their predecessors the mailcoaches and stage waggons, they stopped in many places rather than at one central location. The 'Mobility Bus' used to stop outside the Milk Bar, just west of the Guildhall, but the Pioneer Bus from St Mary Bourne used to stop opposite the Victoria Arms in West Street. As the smaller operators dropped out in the face of competition, a bus station was created out of some old shops in Bridge Street. This sufficed for a time, but it was clear that Andover would need a purpose-built Bus Station, and while a new concrete, two-storey island passenger terminal with large garage building to the rear was being built, the operations of the Wilts and Dorset were carried on from temporary headquarters in Junction Road. The new Bus Station opened in 1951 and Hants and Dorset passengers as well as National Bus Company passengers now arrive and leave Andover from a site symbolically placed next to that reminder of Andover's role in the road transport system of the past, the Town Bridge.

Chapter Thirteen
THE HOSPITAL

'Is any sick? The MAN of ROSS relieves
Prescribes, attends, the med'cine makes and gives;
Despairing Quacks with curses fled the place,'

The casual pedestrian, leaving the Town Centre through the underpass beneath Western Avenue, may be forgiven for not noticing on approaching Junction Road, one of the most charming and bizarre examples of Andover Victorian Rococo. How else can one describe a building whose façade of glazed white and natural red brick within a superfluity of angles and corners, includes windows of most shapes and sizes in wood, stone or brick surrounds, beneath gables of varied height crowned with decorative finials? In 1876, this was the latest fashion and the latest in a series of institutions which in their different ways catered for the sick of Andover.

The earliest of these was a Hospital dedicated to St Mary Magdalene which is mentioned in letters written by Henry III as early as 1249. The earliest mention in Andover's own collection is in 1313 when an exchange of land was made, one acre in the South Field for one acre in the West Field near the 'leper House'. Leprosy was the most feared disease in the Middle Ages, for it disfigured before it eventually killed. Leper houses, or hospitals of St Mary Magdalene were traditionally built away from the main centres of population. In Andover, the west field covered the whole of the slopes between Andover and Abbotts Ann, and here, probably near Gallagher's Copse, stood the Hospital of St Mary Magdalene. The lepers may have made their own cloth, for 'stretchacre' in the West Field suggests a racking ground. The lepers certainly had their own flock of sheep, for in the Chamberlain's accounts for 1471, the men of 'the spetyll' paid 14 pence for a ram from the Church flock.

As the fear of contagion, and the incidence of leprosy decreased, the Spitall lost its primary function as a Hospital and became an almshouse of which mention has already been made. Meantime graver diseases than leprosy had invaded England and some outbreaks had serious results though statistics are lacking. By 1600 the bubonic plague had superseded leprosy as the chief scourge, and medical knowledge at that time had found no remedy for the plague except the sniffing of innocent and ineffective herbs. Nor did the general public have any confidence in surgery. In 1576, William Scullard was summoned by Thomas Kilbery who claimed that he had successfully treated Edmund Scullard by surgery for a skin affliction for which treatment William now refused to pay.

Andover suffered severely from the bubonic plague in 1605. The County Justices had warned the Hundreds that an outbreak was likely. The only effective treatment in the case of an outbreak was isolation, so the conduct of John Robinson, an alehouse-keeper living in lower London Street, is all the more reprehensible for he pretended that the significant 'bubo' or swelling which appeared on his person was an innocent boil and allowed no less than 25 members of various families to enter his house. Within a few days 94 people were affected, and nine separate pest-houses—that is, isolated hospitals—were set up in the fields. Eighteen people died quickly, and 46 were in these pest houses and a further 27 were shut up in two houses in Andover when the Corporation appealed to Sir Henry Whithead J.P. for help. Besides records of burials in gardens and fields, the Town Accounts also record 'William Brexstone payd not his rent in the sickness Tyme behind three half yeares and never kept the shop sinse'.

Not all diseases were cured by medicine or by isolation. Scrofula, an inflammation of the lymphatic gland and a disease of early life was thought to be cured by the magic touch of the King, especially one of the Stuart kings. The parish records contain lists of people who have been touched for the 'King's Evil', and certificates that individuals suffering from the disease had not already been 'touched' were necessary before undergoing this sympathetic magic.

Scientific medicine begins to make an impact during the Eighteenth Century with the introduction of inoculation and notices in the local newspapers give some indication. 'Mr Poore takes this method of informing his friends that he has declined the practice of inoculation and the goods at Pill Farm will be sold as soon as properly aired . . .' appeared in 1770. Evidently Mr Poore still adhered to old fashioned remedies, but in the following year 'Doctor Smith inoculates the small pox at a very convenient house by Weyhill in Hampshire on the usual terms: servants at 2 guineas; coffee, tea and sugar excepted. Patients are taken in at any notice without preparation . . .'

At the same time isolation remained the recognised treatment for small-pox and other diseases. On 3 January 1757, the Corporation decided to erect a Pest-House on a site north of London Lane—now Vigo Road. A chalk wall surrounded the building which at that time stood alone in the East Field. The first resident caretakers were John Thorn and his wife Eleanor who were paid 50/- a year and allowed to use the house and garden. Sometimes the Corporation were less fortunate in their choice of warden. Joseph Pettiford resigned in November 1868 on the grounds of ill-health, and his successor, Charles Stares was removed for misconduct in May 1869.

The Nineteenth Century saw the outbreaks of cholera on several occasions, but these were mostly in the overcrowded conditions of the big urban centres. It occasioned the first legislation for public health, at first merely permissive. In 1872 came the first Public Health Act though some authorities were reluctant to appoint a Medical Officer of Health. St Mary Bourne, under the influence of Dr Joseph Stevens, quickly selected him as M.O.H., while Andover delayed as long as possible, finally appointing in June 1874, Dr S. B. Farr, the Medical Officer to the Board of Guardians of the Poor Law Union, on a fee basis.

The Public Health legislation reflected the public concern on a national level. On a local level an anonymous letter appeared in the 'Andover Chronicle' in January 1872 alleging that the Pest House was being mismanaged and complaining particularly about the inhuman treatment of recent admissions. These allegations were refuted by Dr S. B. Farr. At the same time the Rev H. B. Bousfield, Vicar of Andover wrote to the Borough Council suggesting that the Pest House should be converted to a Cottage Hospital, which suggestion the Council declined to entertain by 7 votes to 3.

Suddenly, in August 1875, the 'Andover Advertiser' announced the building of a Cottage Hospital on a site in Junction Road already provided by Mr Gue, and with the sum of £1,500 already contributed by two benefactors. Members of the public were invited to help with the annual running costs of the new institution on a subscription basis. The first turf was cut by the Vicar on 3 March 1876 and the foundation stone laid on 3 June though not, as advertised, by the Countess of Portsmouth, who was unable to attend, but by Mrs John Loxley, eldest daughter of Sir Charles Pressley who had contributed £1,000 towards the building.

The Council recognised that the Pest House was not in a fit state to be compared with the Cottage Hospital. Changing the name to 'Infectious Hospital' was one step; providing a 'fly' or carriage for the conveyance of small-pox patients, and a shed for the 'fly' was another; preparing plans for alterations was a third, but the most important was a prohibition to the tenant, Mrs French, to take in lodgers. In the end, the Council decided against alterations, but agreed, that the use of the 'Infectious Hospital' and the attendance of a nurse should be free to all patients, but that maintenance and medical attention should be paid by the patient. By comparison, patients at the Cottage Hospital were admitted on the nomination of one of the subscribers, and the figures were reported to the Annual General Meeting. In 1879, the first full year after its completion in January 1878, the Cottage Hospital treated 43 patients from the total population of Andover of about 5,000. Of these, 17 recovered, 2 were sent to other hospitals, 3 left, and 20 benefitted; only one died, of apoplexy having been admitted for an operation on the knee-joint.

Prevention of diseases was a subject of considerable tension in Andover at this time. Before 1872, the earth closet, or privy, was the standard equipment of a tenement, and these were cleaned out by scavengers. Great anxiety was created by an article in the 'Andover Chronicle' for 13 April 1877 in which the discontinuance of scavenging was envisaged. The Urban Sanitary Committee met the following day and recommended that day-work—the collection of household refuse—should be free to all rate-payers, but that night-work—cleaning privies—should be paid for at the rate of 2/6d per closet at houses, and 1/6d per closet at cottages. These charges proved too low and were raised in February 1878. In April 1879, the Surveyor reported that the night-cart was nearly worn out, and was given authority to purchase a new one.

The Pavement Commissioners had been made responsible for draining the town in 1815, and this they had done by making culverts draining into the river, some above and some below the Town Mill. With packed earth as the surface of many of the streets the result was an accumulation of mud in the river which, said Mr Morrant in October 1874, obstructed the working of the Mill. The usual method of clearing the mud was to use a chain harrow which disturbed it enough to cause it to settle further downstream where it spoiled the fishing. Instead of seeking a way of preventing the accumulation of mud, Mr Hammans, one of the Aldermen called attention in August 1875 to the importance of not disturbing the fish spawn by using the chain harrow. Meanwhile Mr Fowle of Upper Clatford Mill offered to keep the river clean from Town Bridge to Upper Clatford for £10 per annum, but after considerable wrangling the Council refused to pay anything.

In January 1880 the Municipal Council was informed by the Local

Government Board that a visit by one of their inspectors to Andover had shown that a new system of drainage was needed. Many houses now had cesspools and a water-borne system of disposal, but these cesspools frequently overflowed causing nuisances and contaminating the river. In March 1880, the Council took appropriate action. They listened to a report from their Surveyor, Alfred Purkess; he suggested that a system of downward intermittent filtration such as at Felstead in Essex—population 8,000—could be installed for less than £2,000. He was instructed to prepare plans, and these were approved and submitted to the Local Government Board in July.

The Council, however, had second thoughts. When Alfred Purkess re-submitted the plans, in June 1881, the Special Drainage Committee decided to check with other boroughs to see what they had done. When the answers were received it was decided to obtain a second opinion for Mr White, Borough Surveyor of Oxford, who said later that if he had known what was involved he would have quoted a higher fee in the first instance. The possibility of a real sewage system, however, led indirectly to the suspension of public bathing in Andover. In August 1882, the Urban Sanitary Committee decided not to open the baths because they needed repair, the season was already advanced, and in any case the land might be needed for the new sewage farm.

Before anything was done, a Mr Child wrote to the Council to find out whether the cost of drainage was to be shared among all the ratepayers or only among those who would benefit. The Town Clerk advised the Council that the matter was being decided in the High Court, which was a good reason for doing nothing. At the same time there was a very powerful influence advocating the continuance of dry-soil techniques. Dr George V. Poore, brother of one of the Council, and son of John Poore (ex-Commander R.N., Alderman, Mayor and founder of Poore's Brewery), Professor of Surgical Medicine at University College, London, with a practice in Wimpole Street, was nevertheless very interested in Andover and rural hygiene. He purchased a large house, Portland House, 21 cottages and a girls' school, and arranged for the night-soil to be collected daily from the dry-closets, and to be spread carefully beneath the surface of his vegetable garden. The crops which were splendid supplied his London home with two baskets of vegetables daily as well as paying the gardener's wages from the surplus sold in the town. In addition to this conservation technique he also advocated the coffinless burial as conducive to improved fertility of the soil. In many ways, G. V. Poore would have been a prophet worth listening

129

to today; perhaps his ideas were the cause of the twenty-year delay, during which Alfred Purkess, the Borough Surveyor, and Inspector of Nuisances, was fully occupied summoning owners or occupiers of property whose cesspools or privies or slaughterhouses or pig-sties proved to be a nuisance to their neighbours, or otherwise busy, since he was also School Attendance Officer, Fire Brigade Engineer and Inspector of Weights and Measures. Nevertheless he continued to revise his plans and estimates for a comprehensive sewage and drainage scheme which the Council were reluctant to implement.

Mr Fowle, having moved upriver to Anton or Pitts Mill continued to press for the removal of mud from the river, and finally brought an action in the County Court in 1896, before His Honour Judge Gye, asking for an order restraining the Corporation of Andover 'from causing or knowingly permitting sewage matter to fall or flow or be carried into the river Anton'. His Honour visited the 'scene of the crime' on two occasions. He had 'no hesitation in saying that the state of the river is very bad. It shows evidence of the strongest possible pollution by sewage.' He would not rely on the witnesses for the defence for he felt that they had inspected the river with their backs to it.

His judgement against the Corporation was suspended for 18 months on condition that steps were taken to end the nuisance, and further suspensions followed as the Corporation slowly continued to make progress. Mr Alfred Purkess's plans were taken out and dusted over, estimates prepared and a contract entered into. Almost at once things went wrong. Pipes with special joints had been ordered, and when they arrived were found to have the wrong connections. The Surveyor collapsed suddenly in 1900 and, though allowed a year's sick leave with pay, was unable to resume duty and retired to Odiham. Mr R. W. Knapp, originally appointed as Deputy Surveyor, succeeded to the vacancy. Meanwhile, the contractors, a Portsmouth firm, ran into further difficulties with sub-surface water and the design of the manholes, and went bankrupt. Some problems were imaginary; in June 1903 a resident in New Street complained of the smell from the ventilating shaft near his cottage. This was odd, because the shaft was not yet connected to the sewer.

Proceedings in the High Court in June 1909 were reported at length in the 'Andover Advertiser' for the Attorney General was suing the Andover Borough Council for polluting the river with sewage from the works in Barlows Lane. The basis for this claim was set forth by J. C. Forster of Clatford Mill who owned a stretch of fishing in the river which had deteriorated badly since 1902, but improved since May 1909. He had first complained to the Council in 1907 when the water in the river was 'perfectly black'. Other witnesses for the prosecution followed and one of the defendants' counsel is reported to have summed up the prosecution's case with these words 'So far as we can gather, when we put the sewage in the river without treatment, the fish were magnificent (laughter). Now they seem to be deprived of something they like and have not been so plentiful since'.

Before the Council's defence was opened, the Judge decided to send Mr Wilson of West Yorkshire to Andover as an impartial investigator to report. In December when the case was resumed, the Judge made no order as Mr Wilson reported that the Council were being very active in the matter. The result of the six days hearing was an undertaking by the Council to 'continue their best endeavours to maintain the efficiency of their sewage works'.

It seems from the evidence which the Council were preparing to bring that most of the pollution came from surface drainage from the roads now being contaminated by oil and petrol, as well as from a gas engine installed in Anton Mill which according to James Beasley who was miller there from 1901 to 1908 turned the water black when it was started up in the morning. One light-hearted incident in the evidence concerned the Public Analyst for Andover, Mr Angell of Southampton. The Council had been forced to appoint him in 1879 after four years of negotiations about salary and fees, but had failed to send him samples for analysis. They had also been unable to dismiss him in 1884 as the Local Government Board refused to allow them to manage without a Public Analyst. In 1909, during the preparation for the High Court action, a bottle labelled 'water collected at the sewage farm' was described by Mr Angell as 'noxious effluvia', whereas it really contained water from the tap at the sewage farm with a little powdered ash and an infusion of garlic. Perhaps the tap water was not entirely free from harmful ingredients.

In accordance with their undertaking in the High Court, the Council came to an agreement with a Westminster consultant Civil Engineer for an improved sewage works on the site of the old Sewage Farm. Further work, repairs and renewals were needed in 1914; the storm water outfall sewer needed attention in 1920; and was the subject of correspondence with the Ministry of Health in 1922; new pumps were ordered in 1926; more money was needed in 1931; another case Lloyd v Corporation in 1936 was fought over sewerage; and further revision and extension of the Sewage Disposal Works took place in 1936.

In the light of all this controversy, it is pleasing to note that in the early stages of Town Development a completely new Sewage Disposal Unit, which the Borough Council sturdily refused to call a Water Purification Plant, was constructed below the limits of habitation in the Anton Valley, and the overflow was carried even further downstream to the junction of the Test and Anton rivers. This was only effected after a proposal by the Borough Council to enlarge the existing works—which was clearly an impossibility— was defeated by the public reaction at an official inquiry held by a Local Government Inspector in February 1966.

The Cottage Hospital continued to be supported by the people of Andover and, even though it was enlarged in 1906 was by 1918 clearly too small for the population. Agreement had been reached with the Rural District Council after considerable negotiation, that an Isolation Hospital should be built to serve both areas at Weyhill in 1910, at which time the Pest House ceased to function.

The ending of the War in 1918 created a new wave of enthusiasm for a hospital, and the task of raising £16,000 to build it was undertaken by a committee chaired by Dr E. A. Farr, son of Dr S. B. Farr and like his father Medical Officer of Health for Andover, and prompted by its secretary Edmund Parsons. To help swell the building fund, a Carnival was organised and the first in 1924 raised £1,300.

Successive Carnivals helped to pay for the building and running of the War Memorial Hospital and after 1948 raised money for other charities. The foundation stone of the Hospital was laid in 1925, and it was opened on 30 June 1926 by Field Marshal the Viscount Allenby. The first name in the Visitor's Book, however, is that of H.R.H. Edward, Prince of Wales, who the previous day visited Enham to open the Landale Wilson Institute. Enham Village Centre was one of many schemes promoted in the last years of the First World War to help rehabilitate those thousands of gas and shell-fire casualties. From basket-work and simple carpentry the Enham Village Centre progressed to a Sheltered Workshop, a unit of production during the Second World War. In 1945 money collected in Egypt as a thank-offering for the victory of El-Alamein, enabled the Village Centre to add facilities for tuberculosis sufferers and the name of the village was changed to Enham-Alamein.

Changes in the health of the nation have meant that the Welfare Workshop can now help other groups of the disabled. For a short time Enham Village Centre worked with the Weyhill Isolation

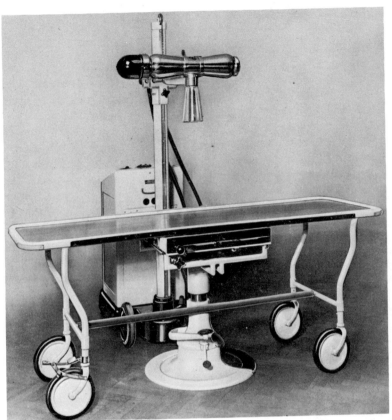

Mobile X-ray unit presented to the gallant defenders of Stalingrad by the people of Andover, 1943. The gift also included a field outfit for processing and viewing X-ray negatives and a portable petrol-electric generator for operating the mobile X-ray unit.

Hospital in caring for tuberculosis patients but the decline in the prevalence of that disease coupled with the almost complete eradication of small-pox means that the Isolation Hospital has lost its 'raison d'être'. The Cottage Hospital lost its original purpose in 1926 and was then used as a Health Centre for many years until the new Health Centre next to the War Memorial Hospital was opened in 1971.

The first mention of fluoridation in Andover is in the minutes of the Public Health Committee which on 8 September 1955 agreed to participate in the Ministry's scheme to study the effects of fluoride in four areas. Although in retrospect it was a storm in a teacup, the campaign proved a traumatic experience for many of those against whom it was directed and split the community to an unprecedented

133

extent. The introduction of 'mass medication' was particularly obnoxious on religious grounds to the small Christian Science group in Andover, who began a campaign against it which had its own diverting moments. For example the Highways and Works Committee refused to divulge on 18 June 1956 any information about the fluoride content of Andover's water supply. Actually it did not begin fluoridation until 17 July 1956. In November the same committee refused to supply to one customer 2 gallons daily of 'wholesome water to which fluoride had not been added' nor allow a rebate from the water rate.

The cause of the Andover Anti-Fluoride Assocation was now taken up by some members of the Council who had originally been in favour and by four Anti-Fluoride Independents elected in May 1957, one of them asking a series of questions under Standing Order 6 about the financial cost of the operation, although it had been made clear from the beginning that all the costs were to be paid by the Ministry. The Chairman of the Finance Committee—perhaps the most powerful post on the Council—tried to take the heat off the Chairman of the Public Health Committee who was the prime target of the campaign. In January 1958 the Attorney-General gave permission for an action against the Council, and in April the Council agreed to end fluoridation after a five year period. This was not enough for the more belligerent members of the A.F.A. who put up more candidates for the Council in all four wards in 1958. With three duly elected, they ousted the two Aldermen, the Chairmen of the Finance and Public Health Committees who were due for re-election, and replaced these key positions with Anti-Fluoride campaigners. On 1 July 1958 the Council decided to stop fluoridation immediately. The High Court action was stayed by an offer not to recommence fluoridation without giving six months notice. The costs of the whole action were paid by the Ministry of Health resulting in some redistribution of the gross national product but not a reduction in the need for dental treatment in Andover. To many people the tragic outcome was not the display of temper at the next Council elections, but the loss to public service of one who, though autocratic, had fought long and hard in the national arena for the rights of small boroughs like Andover.

The Cottage Hospital still stands, though its future use is uncertain. It and the War Memorial Hospital, however, remain as symbols of the determination of the people of Andover to deal with their own health in their own way.

Chapter Fourteen
THE SHOPS

'There London's Voice: "Get Money, Money still"
And then let Virtue follow, if she will".'

The passing of the Andover Hot Pie Shop in 1968 was and is still a matter of regret to many. Its closure symbolised the transition of Andover from a place of local, individual crafts, to an element in a nation-wide commercial complex.

Industry in the very early days of Andover was closely tied to agriculture. Wool merchants bought and sold fleeces and sacks of wool and at a later stage a weaving industry, making kerseys as well as shalloons and serges, was established in Andover as in so many other towns of the Wessex chalkland. Legislation in 1610 attempted to preserve this craft which was threatened by severe competition from other areas. Parchment making was another early craft practised in Andover, but seems to have been overtaken by tanning before the Sixteenth Century. One note remains of a consignment of leather to London in 1575 which totalled 4 cwt and was carried at 2/- per cwt. So important was this commodity that a special court existed to maintain the standard of leather made and sold. All leather was inspected and inferior pieces were condemned by the Triers to whom the poor quality material was brought by the sealers of leather. The profits of sealing leather were leased for a term of years especially during the Eighteenth Century. The proceeds of the sale of unsatisfactory goods were divided between the sealers, the Corporation and the poor.

The Eighteenth Century also saw the establishment of a silk industry in two adjoining premises in London Road near the Walled Meadow; they were mortgaged in 1743 by John Everard as security for payment of a bond, and were still there at the time of the Tithe Award in 1848. The silkweavers lived in a terrace of chalk cottages and their own pub, the Silkweavers' Arms, stood next to their row in Vigo Road until about 1851. That period also witnessed the growth of the service industries which are a feature of so many market

135

J. Smith Esq.   31 December 1879

Dr
to

WALTER PAGE,
Plumber, Glazier, Painter,
AND HOUSE DECORATOR,
GAS FITTER, &c
HIGH STREET,
ANDOVER

ESTIMATES GIVEN FOR GENERAL REPAIRS.

1879
Oct 27 Cleaning off Painting & Varnishing
        to Bath   5 6
Dec 31 To office window — 1 pane ground 20×16   2 6
                                                  8 0

Paid Feb 17th 1880
W Page

towns. Banking was one such. Andover Old Bank which issued its own notes, was owned by William Steele Wakeford, who financed the needs of the builders of the Andover Canal, and who later went into liquidation. Messrs Gilbert and Heath's Bank was working in 1807, though later in 1826 it was Messrs Heath's Bank, and it finally merged with one of the growing national concerns like the Capital and Counties Bank.

Brewing was another industry which most centres of population had acquired by 1800. In place of the individual brewhouses attached to each licensed beerhouse, larger breweries served several houses. Heath's Brewery, opposite Heath's Bank in London Street, and next to Savoy Chambers, was afterwards used as a malthouse to supply other Andover breweries, Hammans Brewery in George Yard, Poore's Brewery in West Street, and Herbert's Brewery in East Street. When these in turn were absorbed by large breweries, some (Heath's and Hamman's) became Steam Laundries, and one (Poore's) a milk depot. No longer is the enticing smell of malt and hops carried on the Andover breeze.

Another industry to be found in every town in the Nineteenth Century was printing. The abolition of a tax on advertisements in 1853 and on newspapers and newsprint in 1855 coincided for-

tunately for Andover with the arrival of the railway. Since no local press was large enough to print a whole newspaper, the first 'local', the 'Andover Advertiser', began as a monthly in 1857 with three pages printed in London and sent down by train, and the front page hand-set and added by a rotary 'mangle' to satisfy a circulation of 1,800–2,000 subscribers. Its success at 2d per copy encouraged the proprietor, John Russell Fox, to change to a weekly paper after seven issues; John Burgiss Brown bought the 'Advertiser' from Fox in 1868 and sold it in 1876 to J. C. Holmes, a bookseller and stationer from Hull but a native of Wimborne who wanted to move back to the south. The Holmes family have been printers in Andover since then and have seen the circulation rise from about 1,000 for an eight page (four printed in London and four printed locally) paper at 1d, to around 18,000 in 1976 for a 9p paper of some 20 pages, all locally produced.

The success of the 'Andover Advertiser' encouraged a rival paper, the 'Andover Times', which began in July or August 1858, published by Frederick J. J. Browne. In an effort to attract more customers, it frequently changed its name; in 1869 the 'North Hants Telegraph', in 1880 the 'Andover Chronicle', then the 'Hampshire Rag' and finally in 1889 the 'Andover Standard'. The exact date of the last 'Andover Standard' is uncertain, for to maintain the title, the proprietors would each week pull a proof of the front page—all advertisements—merely changing the date and send it to Somerset House for registration. The practice ceased about 1912. The printing works were to begin with at 19 High Street, later moved to West Street until demolition in 1968 and now occupy a new building in South Street which bears the name 'Standard Press'.

The mid-Nineteenth Century also saw developments in engineering. In 1855 James Mills sold his small engineering, mill-wrighting and iron foundry at the Acre to Mr Watson of Reading. Some time later, Watson moved the business to a new site in Mylen Road and began manufacturing agricultural machinery. In this he may have been influenced by the success of Robert Tasker and his brother who had established the Waterloo Iron Works at Anna Valley just outside the town limits. Watson's first successful machine was a folding hay elevator, and within a few years production was raised to 150 per annum. A bone crushing mill was developed for export to areas where bone-meal as a fertiliser was required, and when steam ploughing expanded, the firm became large contractors of steam ploughs having at one time 12 sets of equipment for hire. Watson and Haig, from the Acre Ironworks in Mylen Road, now supply spares, and service farm machinery of all sorts.

In the mid-Nineteenth Century the production at the tannery declined, and a new use for the premises was found in October 1895 when a steam laundry was established there by A. E. Welch for the owner W. C. Bracher. After a few years, the Bracher family took complete control and continued it for many years under the name Anton Laundry. The premises include a very fine early Eighteenth Century House which is one of the relics of the tannery period. There was also a mineral water factory in this area in the early part of the present century.

A new business arrived in Andover in 1914 when Hovis Ltd took over the Anton mills. For some time the mills continued to grind flour, but in 1925 flour production was transferred to Bristol, and the animal feeding stuffs plant which had been installed in 1922 was increased. The plant was remodelled in 1953, renamed Vitovis Ltd,—the agricultural subsidiary of Hovis—and is now closed.

The success of the early Hovis plant encouraged McDougall's to take over a milling business established by Mr Fiander in Millway

Road. As a supplement to their London mill, the Andover plant was developed to pack self-raising flour in small quantities. The old mill burnt down in 1925, and although re-built McDougalls seized the chance given by the removal of the Waterworks company next door to take over the well and reservoir. The well supplied water for the wheat-washing plant and the reservoir is an extra source in case of fire. 1953 saw the erection of a large concrete silo clearly visible from the eastern approaches to Andover.

McDougall's mill was converted to electricity in 1929—two years after that form of energy had been introduced to Andover. Lack of an electricity supply had hindered the development of light industry in Andover, though generating plants had been installed in private developments many years earlier. Remains of one such turbine generator remained in the river bed at Cricklade mill until 1976.

When the board of Kelly's Directories Ltd at Kingston-upon-Thames were looking for an alternative site for their developing business, Andover offered several advantages. The Chapel River Press in the Weyhill Road was completed in 1932 and key staff from Kingston were transferred into the main building. Two of Kelly's subsidiary companies transferred from London in 1933 and began production in the western building. There have been continuous improvements at Chapel River Press where many local residents are now employed. The importance of this firm, however, is that it was the first non-local business to be established in Andover. Previous enterprises had been either associated with agriculture, milling, farm machinery, or with a market town, banking, brewing and printing. 1932 marks the start of the industrialisation of Andover.

The reasoning behind 'town development' was the need of the London County Council to persuade firms to move from the crowded streets of the metropolis to the undeveloped areas along the railway lines. The 1952 Town Development Act gave the powers necessary to base development upon an existing town rather than create a town *de novo*. In Hampshire, the County Council were prepared to help the London County Council to develop the two towns of Basingstoke and Andover, both of which are sited at a convenient distance along the main Waterloo–Exeter railway.

The Town Development plan allocated two large areas, one at Walworth on the east, the other at Portway on the west, on which factories of various sizes could be built for companies wishing to transfer all or part of their London business to a more attractive and rural setting. At the same time arrangements were made for housing, schools and shops for the increased population.

The new factories are evidence of the progress made in the industrial growth of Andover. In 1961 there were grave doubts in the minds of many inhabitants as to the desirability of such development. The Drill Hall was packed when a protest meeting was held and an Anti-Overspill Committee was formed to nominate and support candidates in all wards of the Borough at the next Municipal Elections, pledged to prevent the implementation of the scheme. Four thousand signatures were obtained to a document objecting to the new Town Map for Andover which allocated land for the development. Many people believed that these tactics would defeat town development just as similar tactics had reversed the decision to add fluoride to the town's water supplies, particularly since many of the leaders of the victorious Anti-Fluoride Association were prominent in the Anti-Overspill movement.

The controversy, however, was conducted with admirable restraint on both sides. When the Anti-Overspill candidates were defeated at the elections and the Minister approved the Town Map after a hearing of objections which lasted for six weeks, all organised opposition to town development ceased. One of the significant factors missing in the later campaign was the religious and moral objections which had stirred up the earlier opposition.

The new companies which have moved to Andover and their employees have created an increase in the numbers of Chartered Accountants, Insurance Brokers, Employment Agencies, Banks, Building Societies, and other 'service industries'. Office accommodation provided in the new shopping precinct allows large departments of the Ministry of Social Security and the Ministry of Employment to deploy their resources fully. In addition to the large multiple stores provided in the shopping centre, others have been built on redeveloped sites in the High Street.

The net result of the industrialisation of Andover has been to create a greater choice of employment. Whereas many school leavers were forced to seek employment away from home, they should now, industrial recessions permitting, be able to find some occupation locally which will not only employ all their talents but provide them with a satisfying future even though multiple stores and multi-storey office blocks do not, in the opinion of some of the more elderly inhabitants of the area, compensate for the loss of old, long-established, privately owned businesses.

Chapter Fifteen
THE HOUSES

'Cutler saw tenants break, and houses fall,
For very want, he could not build a wall'.

The face of Andover has changed radically during the last ten years; perhaps more radically than in any other ten year period, and yet as each new estate is built with its ring road and pedestrian ways it creates an environment for its inhabitants which in its freedom from wheeled traffic is similar to the earliest settlement, 'aet Andeferan'. About the houses in which the earliest townsfolk dwelt there is little which can be said. They were built of wood and mud with a thatch roof and burned easily; fresh houses were built on the same site thus complicating any evidence for the earlier dwelling. Neither the first house nor its replacement had a foundation but rested directly on a packed earth floor and so the only traces would be the holes which took the corner posts of the house.

Some such holes have been found in the course of redevelopment, but it was not possible to relate them to a single structure. Early deeds give little help. One deed of about 1290 conveys a hearth and courtyard which is part of a large tenement, and is 29 feet wide on the south. Another deed dated 1343 conveys a piece of land between one house and the yard of another house, the dimensions being '8 feet long and 20 feet broad'. Winchester College possesses an early lease of a 'shop 22 feet in depth, 12 feet in frontage and with the right of opening a door into the other part of the tenement and the use of the well therein' for an annual rent of 10/-.

The first recorded Fire of Andover was in 1141. Rebuilding was no real hardship for Harewood and Finkley Forests provided plenty of wood. Many of the houses would have been of the simple cruck type, but some might have been of the more sophisticated timber-frame construction, which could be built quite quickly from standardised components, the maximum length being only 20 feet. Lengths of more than 20 feet became inceasingly difficult to obtain after the 'Great Fire of Andover of 1435'. The effective width of a

141

house thereafter, limited as it was by the length of the available timber, was about 16 feet, but its length was more variable, since beams could be joined together to make the longer rails on which the joints of the upper floors rested. About 10 foot was the standard length of a bay, and a 'five-bay' house would therefore be about 50 feet long by 12 to 16 feet wide. The nature of the houses suggest that Andover was an untidy place, with gable ends facing the street, each bay of the building possibly housing a different tenant, and a narrow alley between the buildings to afford access. With no water-supply in pipes, no sanitation, no street-cleaning and dustbin-emptying service, conditions in Andover must have been no more pleasant than those of the rural dweller.

Only one of the buildings from the mid-Fifteenth Century rebuilding of Andover survives in part, behind the refaced front and side of the Angel Inn. Of the Sixteenth Century houses, 2 Chantry Street has been modernised for residential purposes, 90 High Street became an antique shop, now closed, Ford Cottage at the foot of Chantry Street remains to prevent the modernisation of the garage premises which surround it, and the Lamb Inn in Winchester Street is a much mutilated example of a late Sixteenth Century design. As the price of timber rose rapidly during this period, it became customary to re-use timber from demolished houses, and it is probable that many of the buildings in Andover of later periods contain considerable amounts of timber originally used in much earlier buildings.

The same technique of cannibalisation is even more apparent in the case of stonework. The only local stone, flint, is not a satisfactory walling material even when expertly knapped. Some of the stone used in building the Bell Inn in 1534 came from Selborne Priory which was being demolished. Thirteenth Century dressed stone-work was found to have been re-used in the foundations of 81 High Street (Sixteenth Century, now demolished) and 37 High Street (Seventeenth Century, also demolished) though much of the foun-dations of the latter were of brick.

Brick-making in Andover probably began about 1500, very likely in Old Winton Road, formerly Brick-kiln Street. The brickwork of the 'Bell' (1534) was expertly laid, implying that local craftsmen were skilled in the manufacture and use of this comparatively new building material. By 1550 flint and mortar walls seem to have become unfashionable, and replaced in both chimney stacks and cellars by brickwork. The wall panels between the timber framing were still of wattle and daub infill as late as 1700 when the old 'Folly

Inn', demolished in 1969, was built, though by the Seventeenth Century this technique was being replaced by brick infill or 'nogging'.

The principal hazard of the town dweller was still fire. With houses roofed with thatch and placed so close together—the size of the original house plots can still be seen in some parts of the High Street where frontages of 20 feet occur regularly—any unguarded sparks could set light to a whole section of the town, as indeed happened in 1647. Earlier and probably as a result of the 1435 fire, the Gild Merchant had bought a number of leather buckets to be kept in the Guildhall and used for putting out fires. The courts recognised the problem and fined those whose chimneys or 'flews' were faulty although that was no solution. The churchwardens also provided leather buckets, (one purchase was recorded in June 1747) and crooks to remove the burning thatch, and the Trading Companies which succeeded the Guild Merchants also provided leather buckets at various times in the Eighteenth Century.

During the Eighteenth Century, Fire Insurance became a common feature of town life, each Insurance Company organising a team of fire-fighters to try to save houses insured by the company. The first fire-engine in Andover was owned by the Sun Fire Insurance Co and was used from 1717 onwards to protect premises, known by the plaque on the wall, to be insured by that Company. The engine, and another purchased by a rival company, were housed in a shed provided by the vestry, where they were in a central position in the town. This 'Fire Station' was a pub, 'The Silent Man', opposite 'The Angel' and next door to the Norman Gate.

Eighteenth Century houses in Andover are mostly to be found in the central area. In the High Street, the Star and Garter Hotel has a fine façade of the latter part of the century with a Venetian window and one non-window which has caused window-cleaners and landlords to disagree. It is usually suggested that the blocking of windows was caused by the window-tax first imposed in 1696 and not removed until 1851. All houses paid a basic 2/- a year with additions according to the number of windows. Details of the tax in Andover are few; one, however, is a letter to the Collectors certifying that as Charles Westcombe's house was burnt to the ground in February 1697, 'there is noe dwelling house there to paye the sayd tax for'.

Since the townspeople have never been rich by external standards there are no outstanding examples of buildings of beauty or architectural merit, but there are a few of pleasing aspect. East Street has a fine terrace of late Eighteenth Century houses, and the Katherine Wheel in Bridge Street, now part of the Council offices, has an Eighteenth Century structure concealed behind numerous improvements. Another fine early example (1742) is the now-vandalised Headmaster's House attached to the old Grammar School where broken glass and bird droppings contrast with the gracious proportions of the rooms and the splendid elegance of the staircase so similar to the Phoenix in Chantry Street which was demolished in 1968. There might have been more houses of that period remaining if a bonfire in 1811 had not got out of hand and started a smaller version of the Great Fire. Fortunately, the presence of a number of French Prisoners-of-War meant that a virile source of power was at hand—so many of the younger men of Andover, like Midshipman Poore, being elsewhere engaged during those years. As a result of their efforts, the exiles were afterwards more readily accepted by the conservative and chauvinistic, if not xenophobic, Andover people.

The whole episode showed the need for co-operation in fire-fighting, but the Corporation and the new Town Council were equally reluctant to commit themselves to any expenditure. After delaying for many years, the Town Council finally brought themselves to agree to pay for the Fire Brigade from the Borough Rate in 1860, but failed to spend any money until the formation of an Andover Volunteer Fire Brigade in 1867 under Superintendent P. H. Poore. The Council then agreed to purchase another fire engine from Shand and Mason at a cost of £178, and took no further interest in the Fire Brigade until 1879.

The destruction of Hurstbourne Priors House at Christmas 1870 was not entirely the fault of the Andover Brigade, for when the members assembled in the High Street with the engine, the livery stable keeper declined to supply the horses which had only just returned from an all-day engagement. For an hour the argument continued in the frosty High Street until horses were obtained from another source. The delay may have been decisive, for the house was completely destroyed.

The public Health Act of 1875 contained among its other clauses provision for the supply of piped water to hydrants in urban areas. There was, of course, no Water Company at that time, and as the Town Council made no attempt to remedy the deficiency a private Waterworks Company was established with 62 shareholders holding 800 £5 shares. The bulk of the shares, 528, were held by Andover residents, 135 were held by residents in the villages around Andover, 45 in London, 35 in Salisbury and the rest from Devizes,

Heading of Insurance Policy.

Marlborough, Basingstoke and Hailsham. Mr Frederick Ellen, an estate agent, was the first elected Chairman of Directors, and Mr F. J. J. Browne, of the 'Andover Standard' was the Secretary. The land for a reservoir was purchased from B. Hawkins in Millway Road, together with the lease of a bore-hole on the land next to it. A pumping engine was obtained from Messrs Ness and Mimms of Winchester, the contract for the reservoir went to F. E. Beale, and the contract for laying the 3″ water main to Thomas Butt. The Directors offered to provide 50 hydrants and to keep them in repair for £50 per annum and this the Town Council accepted.

The Fire Brigade now needed reorganising, or at least re-shaping to meet the facilities provided by the fire hydrants. A report on the state of the Fire Brigade printed in the 'Andover Advertiser' on 11 July 1879 showed that while the Shand and Mason engine was in excellent condition, and the late 'Sun' engine good, engine nos 3 and 4 being small, needed repainting and removal from the shed in the churchyard. The Finance Committee report printed on 10 October showed also that the engines were not being cleaned and the rules and regulations of the Fire Brigade were being neglected. Furthermore, while the public expressed their thanks for the work of the Fire Brigade, no records appeared to have been kept of the fires attended or of the costs of attendance.

On 14 October, Superintendent Poore resigned, and John Moore, Assistant Superintendent, resigned also. On 6 November the resignation of all the other members of the Volunteer Fire Brigade was received, though they did offer to continue to act. Temporarily, the Mayor became Superintendent, and the Borough Surveyor added the Fire Engineer's hat to the others he wore. As Manager of the Waterworks he supervised the installation of hydrants to the instructions of the Borough Surveyor (himself) so that the Fire Brigade (of which he was Engineer) could deal with fires, the water-carts could draw supplies to lay the dust for the Surveyor of Highways (himself) or to carry out necessary flushing ordered by the Inspector of Nuisances (another of his hats).

Two large mid-Victorian houses of this period which have not been destroyed either by neglect or in the name of re-development, stand in Weyhill Road. Rookwood, now a girls' school, was earlier called Highfield and was the home of the Poore family. During the Inter-War period it was the home of Lord John Joicey Cecil, one of the Borough Council during that period, who insisted on wearing a 'boater' throughout the year. Beech Hurst, built by the Town Clerk Harry Footner about 1850 was, in 1900, the home of Charles A. Swinburne, a barrister and collector of water-colours and etchings—his catalogue of them was privately published—which hung from massive hooks which can still be seen in the principal rooms. During the Second World War it was a home for convalescent officers, and after the war became the headquarters of the Andover Borough Council and, for a time, of the Southampton Water Board in the additional office space which was added. It is now the administrative headquarters of the Test Valley Borough, while the Technical Services Department of the Test Valley has taken over the old Rural District Council Offices in Junction Road.

There are several ways of tracing the development of the town in the late Nineteenth Century. The Minutes of the Waterworks Company show where additional supplies were required, sometimes specifically for building purposes, occasionally for agricultural but most often for domestic. Letters asking for an extension of the 3″ mains for a further 20 or 50 yards suggest new developments. Special arrangements were made for Junction Station which required enormous quantities of water. So important were the Waterworks, that the Town Council offered to buy the Company, valued at £8,100 in July 1883 for £7,500, but after the offer had been accepted, the Council withdrew. The Company sank another well and installed an 8 h.p. (silent) Otto Gas Engine. This was too noisy, so an 8 h.p. steam engine was purchased and the number of hours of daily pumping increased to provide adequate pressure. Finally in 1890, the Company went into voluntary liquidation, and was acquired by the Council for £6,500. Nevertheless the proprietors received £7.5.5d. for each £5 share and this together with annual dividents of up to 7% meant that over the 16 years period an original investment of £5 would have almost doubled to £9.19.4d.

In the summer of 1881 a new facility arrived in Andover, the Telephone. The Highways Committee were disturbed to find that unsightly poles were being erected between Weyhill Tavern and Mr Gibbons' office in Bridge Street, in places on the outside of the pavement. The Committee decided that iron poles would be less likely to break and ordered these to be placed on the inner edge of the pavement, but expressed concern about the problem of damages if the pole should fall or the wire should break. The following month their concern extended, at last, to the pedestrian and they requested that the Telephone Posts should be painted white up to a height of 6 feet. It might have been better to have added more street lights, but this would have been expensive. The installation of a telephone was a luxury for the very few, and when in 1899 the Town Clerk was instructed by the Council to write to the authorities about connection to the Trunk system, there were in fact only sixteen subscribers to the National Telephone Company.

Much of the late Victorian period building has been demolished in the course of re-development, but there are still some examples left. The practice of adding a stone bearing a date to the façade of a group of houses helps considerably in identifying them. The Victoria Park estate is of this period and other dated buildings are the Masonic Hall in East Street (1885), Pevensey Cottages in New Street (1896), Gloucester Terrace in Charlton Road (1888) and Hazel Villas in Junction Road (1885).

The Fire Brigade was reorganised in 1880 with many of the same members as before and seems to have been as effective as its motive power allowed. Arrangements were made to hire horses when needed at 2 guineas, and when the owner abruptly raised the price of 3 guineas in January 1882, an alternative supply was quickly found. Details of the fires attended are noted after 1892, but out of the first 70 recorded fires, only 18 were within the borough.

In September 1895, the Brigade was called to a fire at Whitchurch which the local fire engine could not deal with because it was disabled. Despite the assistance also of the 'Basingstoke Steamer' which came by rail, the shop was destroyed. Cottonworth Farm at Fullerton had fires in August 1893, August 1895 and October 1897 on each occasion being caused by sparks from the railway setting fire to a rick. Overheated chimneys, sparks from a bakehouse and a forge are among the causes known, though lightning is assumed to have hit a straw rick at Pavey's Farm in September 1896. In most instances the Brigade arrived too late to do more than try to save what had not yet been caught alight. There was great indigation when on 10

January 1900 the Pavilion on the Recreation Ground was completely gutted.

Edwardian developments in Andover can be traced mainly through the date-stones on buildings, but also through the records of the Council's Water-works Committee, or the Urban Sanitary Committee which dealt with planning and building bye-laws. Named and dated houses of this period are Port Arthur Cottages in New Street (1904, when else), Cromwell in Junction Road (1909), 'The Pollens' in Charlton Road (1910) and the Drill Hall in East Street (1905).

The Waterworks entered an increasingly difficult period with the spread of housing. One of the first ideas put forward by the new Manager, the Borough Surveyor, Mr R. W. Knapp, was of a reservoir on Bere Hill which would supply all the town by a gravity feed. He put forward the idea in 1900, but it was not until 1911 that the Council authorised conversations about acquiring a suitable site. In 1912, the Council approved a scheme for a half-million gallon reservoir on Bere Hill but refused to buy the land needed. In the meantime the demand for water continued to increase, and the pumps were driven for longer hours, creating more noise and nuisance, and even so there were complaints about insufficient supplies. In 1917 the Colonel in charge of the new Aviation Station on the western outskirts of the town complained about the price of water supplied to him. Finally, the Council agreed to purchase 3 acres for £50 in March 1918 and another 5 acres for £200 in April 1918. This done, the grazing on these acres were promptly let to a farmer.

Repeated complaints about the noise of the pumps now being driven continuously, activated the council into a decision to install an electric pump when electricity became available. Discussions began in December 1925, the contract was signed in March 1926 and the new engine connected to the well in October 1927. Surprisingly it was so efficient that it sucked the well dry, and could not be restarted without re-priming. To change the electric pump from the outer well to the inside well which was deeper, and to sink it below the level of the water took until December 1928. In 1929 water charges were increased; from 1/- to 1/6 per cow per quarter, for example, and non-domestic rates up to 2/- per 1,000 for the first 10,000 gallons.

After years of prevarication the Council finally decided to revise the existing situation. They appointed Messrs Lemon and Blizard of Southampton as Consulting Engineers to draw up a comprehensive scheme. It is possible that a letter received by the Town Clerk from the Unemployment Grants Committee, read to the Council on 20 December, stating that grants would be available to help with expenditure on water schemes, may have affected the Council's decision. The new plans occupied the attention of the Waterworks Committee, enlarged to include the whole of the Town Council, until the opening of the Smannell Road works on 19 October 1932 by the Mayor, Alderman H. J. Humber, J.P., who had been Chairman of the Waterworks Committee for many years. In fact the supply from the new boreholes in Smannell Road had been used since April 1932 to supplement the dwindling supply from the Millway Road wells.

During the first year the saving in the cost of supplying water was £450; by 1937 the cost had been cut from 2.24d per 1,000 gallons in August 1932 to a mere $\frac{1}{2}$d. The old Millway Road site was finally sold to McDougall's in March 1936, and the money received was spent in doubling the capacity of the Bere Hill reservoir, so that there was three days supply in hand. The Council steadily refused to supply water to outlying districts through the 3″ water main, though they would send the water-cart round at 2/- per 1,000 gallons. Not many householders were able to store that quantity, so few took advantage of the offer. When Enham faced a water crisis in 1937, the Council were sympathetic but unhelpful. Their major concern during this period was to trace the leaks in the water main, and finally they succeeded in cutting the night-loss down to about 4,000 gallons an hour.

Council Housing schemes started in 1926 with a contract for the erection of 24 houses in Batchelors Barn Road and a further 24 in Vigo Road, which are easily identifiable. The Housing Act of 1930 allowed for compulsory purchase of property for Slum Clearance and many Clearance Orders were made between 1931 and 1939, resulting in the demolition of the older and unsuitable houses in Chantry Street, New Street, Vigo Road and South Street. At the same time, the Council was building houses on the Drove Estate, now King George's Road, in a piece-meal fashion, 60 houses in 1934–5, 18 more in 1938, another 14 in 1938–9 and so on.

From 1893 to 1936 Arthur Beale was associated with the Fire Brigade, for many years its Captain and keeper of records. A disastrous fire at some thatched cottages in New Street in 1901 attracted the national press and in the following year, call bells were installed in the homes of firemen who had previously been summoned by a bugle, or by a hand-operated hooter. In 1904 the Brigade acquired a 'steamer' which unfortunately was trapped on its first outing at the level crossing gate. On the other hand, at Whitsun 1914 a team of Andover firemen won the National Shield for hose cart drill. A new fire engine was purchased in 1921 and housed in the East Street Fire Station next to the Masonic Hall which enabled the Brigade to serve its wide district rather faster, if conditions allowed. But the cold was so intense at the Heronry, Tufton, on 9th December 1933 that water froze on the firemens' uniforms which had to be chipped free before they could move from the hosepipes, and in May 1936 drought prevented them from saving the New House, Wildhern. In 1939 the Andover brigade was merged with the Auxiliary Fire Service and equipped with one of the familiar Dennis engines in 1941. After the War, the Hampshire Fire Brigade built a new Fire Station at the top of London Street where a few full-time and some part-time firemen maintain the traditions of their predecessors.

After 1945, there was an attempt to form a Housing Association to provide houses for sale to members and the Council continued to build rentable property here and there as opportunity offered. Cherry Tree Road, Suffolk Road and others were added to the town map. In the circumstances, restricted resources and unimaginative design, it is not surprising that so many of these houses are basically identical, differing only in the amount of embellishment lavished upon them by their occupiers.

A chance to make a radical change came with Town Development. New estates were planned as complete entities with traffic-free centres and a ring road to provide access. Imaginative groupings and plantings became possible even though the standard unit was identical. Some of the new estates were sufficiently impressive to merit Civic Design awards, but the standard of construction in some cases meant that maintenance became expensive.

The problems associated with housing and industrial development on such a large scale and with so many authorities involved can only be solved by agreement between the various departments concerned. It is to the credit of Andover that regular meetings of all the relevant Heads of Departments of the three authorities, (Architects, Housing, Water, Drainage, Highways, Parks, Planning, Finance, Education and so on) with various Consultants, took place in Andover to monitor the progress and sort out the difficulties before they became pressing. This 'Management Team' method was evolved early in the expansion of Andover and though it could not prevent such consequences as the building of houses with a tendency to allow water to penetrate, it enabled the development to proceed in accordance with a time schedule.

Chapter Sixteen
THE HISTORIANS

Full in the passage of each spacious gate,
The sage Historians in white garments wait;
Grav'd o'er their seats the form of Time was found,
His scythe revers'd, and both his pinions bound.

It would be impossible to close this nostalgic account of Andover without paying tribute to those whose diligent care preserved the documents which in time became archives, as well as to others who have transcribed them, or commented on facets of Andover's past. The people of Andover have most cause to be grateful to King Edgar and to his successors the Kings of England who gave the town its peculiar status; to the men of the Gild Merchant who caused the results of their deliberations to be recorded; to the members of the old Corporation whose financial needs required them to preserve their rights; to the compilers of the 'Great Book of Andover' begun in 1574 in which were recorded all the property transactions of the Corporation until enthusiasm evaporated in 1653; and to the first elected members of the Municipal Corporation who asked William Henry Walter Titheridge, an Inspector of Weights and Measures, to examine the manuscripts in the Town Chest to decide which properties rightfully belonged to the Town and which to the newly created Charity Commissioners.

In the course of compiling his lists of property, W. H. W. Titheridge copied extracts from the earliest Minute Books, and these are invaluable evidence, as the first three books (Liber 'A', Liber 'B' and Liber 'C') are now missing. To these extracts, copied again in part, he added other notes in a manuscript book entitled *Materials for a History of Andover*. Not much was known at that time of the prehistoric and Roman periods, but such as was known was incorporated. Though it was unfinished, to him goes the honour of being the first to attempt a comprehensive History of Andover. A few years later Rev J. S. Pearsall wrote the *Historical Memorials of a Christian Fellowship* in which he described the early vicissitudes of the Non-Conformists in Andover.

So important was Titheridge's report, that the Borough Treasurer, Samuel Shaw copied out the whole report in 1856. He also left behind him a number of volumes in which he made notes on trade and gilds, parliamentary representation of Andover, lists of Bailiffs and Mayors from Edward I to 1870 together with notes on various local families, Sandys, Wallop, Wynn, Henley, West, Withers, and others. In addition to these eight small octavo volumes, there is a collection of printed articles which Shaw made up for binding, and which is on the shelves of the Library Local Collection. One of these articles his own special interest, for it is an offprint from his paper printed in the Numismatists' Journal recording the finding of an Anglo-Saxon coin in 1854. The coin, now in the British Museum, is unique in that the name of the King, Beorhtric of Wessex, and the name of the moneyer, Penochtun are otherwise both unknown. Shaw's contemporary, Dr Joseph Stevens of St Mary Bourne, though principally concerned with his own valley, nevertheless excavated Roman buildings on Castle Hill and Finkley within Andover's boundaries.

In 1880 the Rev Charles Collier became vicar of Andover and, being a keen antiquarian, he approached the Council for permission to consult the Archives. This was somewhat reluctantly given, and Canon Collier began the systematic publication of some of the documents. Sometimes these appeared in the pages of the 'Andover Advertiser' but the first pamphlet was a transcription of the Churchwardens' Accounts for 1470–3. In this he was assisted by Rev Robert Hawley Clutterbuck, the Rector of Knight's Enham who was more of an archaeologist than a historian. The two men also made a survey of 'The Charters and Grants of Andover' which was also printed by Holmes. In 1890 Clutterbuck became Rector of Penton Mewsey and despite his failing health devoted himself to the antiquities of the Hampshire-Wiltshire border. Two years after he died in 1896, some of his work was published by Bennett Brothers of the Salisbury Journal under the title *Notes on the parishes of Fyfield, Kimpton, Penton Mewsey, Weyhill and Wherwell.* Some thirty pages of this work are devoted to the quarrel between the Corporation of Andover and William Drake over the Weyhill Fair, and it also includes extracts from the missing Minute Book, Liber 'C'.

Collier's and Clutterbuck's interest in the history of Andover was passed on to the Organist of St Mary's Church, Arthur C. Bennett, and to Edmund Parsons of the firm of Parsons and Hart. In 1920 these two collaborated on a *History of the Free Grammar School of Andover, latterly called Andover Grammar School,* under which title they not only listed the Benefactors, the Benefactions, the Buildings, the Schoolmasters, the Scholars and the New Management, but also anything else that took their fancy like the Reform of the Calendar 1752 (from which they drew the wrong inference), the Voyage of Robert Tomson 1553–1568, the Residents in Andover between the ages of 12 and 70 in 1582, and not least the mistakes occurring on the Benefactions Tablet. Among such interest material they included transcripts of various wills and two inventories, one of 1611 and the other of 1624 which indicate the furbishings expected in a middle-class or professional household in the early Seventeenth Century, now an increasingly common field of study for historians.

Arthur Bennett had already published a History of Music in Andover in weekly instalments in the 'Andover Advertiser' in 1901 and in 1921–2 he contributed a series of articles relating to the administration of the Poor Law in Andover and Whitchurch—a field in which he was a pioneer. About 1900 he compiled some notes on the History of St Mary's Church which was expanded into a guide book, the first edition being published from Gloucester in 1933. The present edition is the 9th. He also wrote articles on the History of the Bell Inn, the plague in Andover, the King's Evil, Prisoners of War and Refugees.

Edmund Parsons also produced articles on Andover's past. These were usually given as lectures to local societies, then printed by the 'Advertiser' in parts and finally set up in pamphlet form. His work was mainly on the Middle Ages: the 'Manor' (1924), 'Charters' (1925), 'Gild of Merchants' (1925), 'Court Rolls of the Hundred' (1934), 'Ordination Deed of the Chantry' (1935), the 'Andover Woollen Industry' (1946) and an 'Etymological Schedule of Place Names in the Andover District' (n.d.) During this period he was writing to many other sources for information on such subjects as Andover, Massachussetts; Bishops' Registers; Cold Harbour; the Heath family, and compiling copious notes which he added to those of his colleague Bennett, in preparation for the History of Andover which they were going to write. These notes deal mostly with Andover between 1200 and 1700 and the great events like the War Memorial Hospital—which he and Dr Farr virtually founded—which was based on the design of his own house Tyhurst in Winchester Road, he passed over as too recent.

The destruction of priceless archives during war-time under the guise of saving waste paper, and to reduce fire-risk in the event of bombing, prompted the formation of the National Register of Archives whose primary function was to help those areas where

Record Offices had not been established. In 1951 a trained archivist, J. B. Morgan, was employed to catalogue the existing archives belonging to the Town Council, and for many years this was the only list and useful for its details of the early Latin deeds. A branch of the National Register of Archives was established in Andover in 1957 and spent many happy evenings cataloguing the deposits in the parish chests in the surrounding area. The group continued to meet and discuss the local history of Andover maintaining an interest which for many of them had been stimulated by Edmund Parsons, During this period Hubert W. Earney, the local Manager of the Southern Evening Echo produced a very successful book on the *Inns of Andover* (1st edition 1955, 2nd edition 1971) and Stella M. Longstaff, Senior Mistress of the Grammar School from 1925 to 1950, wrote a shortened version of Bennett and Parsons book which she not only improved by reduction but brought up to date.

Outsiders were taking an interest in Andover's past. Bernard R. K. Paintin wrote an account of Methodism in Andover under the title 'Since Wesley Came' and this was published to mark the bicentenary of Methodism in Andover in 1951 by Holmes. The career of Sir Francis Blake Delaval M.P. for Andover 1754 to 1768 forms a major part of *The Gay Delavals* by Francis Askham, published by Jonathan Cape in 1955. L. T. C. Rolt was commissioned to write a history of the *Waterloo Iron Works*, an account of Taskers' Brothers Foundry at Little Ann, published by David and Charles in 1969. Ian Anstruther researched and explained the *Scandal of the Andover Workhouse*, (Godfrey Bles) in 1973.

The crucial date in the career of the 'History of Andover' was 1968, for the Town Clerk informed a meeting of the Local Archives Committee (then a branch of the N.R.A.) that the plans for the new Public Library included the provision of an archival room, and he questioned whether this room would be justified unless some local use could be made of the documents. The Committee were able to report that they had started preparing a series of pamphlets on Andover's past primarily for educational use, but also as a preliminary to the full-scale study contemplated by Titheridge and others. The first series of pamphlets was produced fairly quickly: between 1968 and 1970 pamphlets on 'The Corporation of Andover' (1599–1835) (M. J. Darrah), 'The North West Hampshire Labourer, 1867–75' (George E. Brickell). 'Timber-Framed Building in Andover' (Richard Warmington), 'The Andover-Redbridge Canal', 'The New Poor Law in 1845', 'The Inclosure of Andover Common Fields 1785', and 'A Register of the Unreformed Corporation' (1599–1835) were produced in quarto size.

A second series of pamphlets, now in A4 size, consist mainly of collections of shorter articles in 'Test Valley and Border Anthology'. In addition, longer studies of the 'Whitchurch Workhouse' (A. C. Bennett reprint), 'The Bell Inn' (Richard Warmington) and 'The Andover Hundred in 1086', have been issued together with reprints of the earlier pamphlets on 'The North West Hampshire Agricultural Labourer in 1845 and 1867–75' in one issue. A series of printed pamphlets was also commissioned by the Local Archives Committee beginning with 'Men of Andover' (H. W. Earney, 1971), 'Members of Parliament for Andover 1295–1885' (R. Arnold Jones, 1972) and 'The Community of Andover before 1825' (Melville T. H. Child, 1972). 'Andover in Hampshire' (1969) and 'Andover, Men, Money and Manners in Early Times' (1970) written and published by Melville Child, although not under the aegis of the Local Archives Committee, were like 'The Community of Andover', anthologies of the past. To celebrate 150 years, Dr Barrington White and the Revd Walter Fancutt wrote 'The Story of Andover Baptist Church 1824–1974'. Realising the need for a brief account, the Deputy Librarian, Elizabeth Watthews compiled a chronological account of Andover in 1969, which she later expanded into a small duplicated booklet in 1971 which ran into a second edition in 1973. When the end of the Borough of Andover was imminent, the Council decided to employ Mrs M. E. Griffiths, late of the Hampshire Record Office, to catalogue the vastly increased collection of documents loosely called the 'Archives'. The new catalogue contains 479 pages and is admitted by its compiler to be lacking in details in places.

Rising costs have put printed publications beyond the Local Archives Committee's financial capacity unless some help can be found from outside sources. 'A Short History of Andover' was produced in 1976 for use in classrooms particularly by the 9 to 13 age group with the aid of a generous grant from the Andover Charter Trustees.

EPILOGUE

'A perfect Judge will read each work of Wit
With the same spirit that its author writ:
Survey the WHOLE, nor seek slight faults to find
Where nature moves, and rapture warms the mind'.

This portrait of Andover was not compiled without a great deal of pleasure and help. Acknowledgements must be made first to the late Charter Trustees, successors to Andover Borough Council, and to their Clerk, Clive M. Burton for permission to consult and quote from those fascinating relics of the past which the ever willing Library staff brought blinking into the daylight from the dark confines of the stacks. Similar acknowledgements of gratitude for permission to consult and quote from the County Records are tendered to the County Archivist and her staff. To George E. Brickell, for many years Secretary of the Local Archives Committee, Melville T. H. Child, whose command of palaeography makes sense out antique scribblings, and John Whatley, former Town Clerk of Andover, who guided my steps through the hazards of composition, to the Revd R. W. Bridle who kindly criticised the first draft of Chapter Three, to all my friends and colleagues on the Local Archives Committee, past and present including Richard Arnold Jones, Ernest W. Bryant, former Librarian of Andover, the late Jack Davis who dreamed of seeing a History of Andover, Hubert W. Earney of the 'Southern Evening Echo', Martin Loveridge, whose collection of Andoveriana is enviable, C. J. Padwick, Derek J. Tempero of the 'Andover Advertiser', to Sandra Harvey who typed the final draft, to Associated Book Publishers who turned the script into a book free of charge, but above all to Pat Simmonds whose idea this was and who with John Isherwood kept it going, I tender my thanks. None of them is responsible, alas, for any errors or omissions which I have made.

JOHN SPAUL
Longparish, Andover 1977.

INDEX OF VERSES

The verses by Alexander Pope which head each chapter can be found in the following works:

SELECTIVE, CONCISE INDEX OF LOCAL NAMES

The names in this list are of inhabitants of Andover, Charlton and Penton unless otherwise stated.

159